Shadows & Verse

Shadows & Verse

Classic Dark Poems with Celebrity Commentary

EDITED BY
Jonathan Maberry

Edited by Jonathan Maberry

SHADOWS & VERSE: CLASSIC DARK POEMS WITH CELEBRITY COMMENTARY

Copyright © 2024 Jonathan Maberry Productions
All poems are in the public domain

All rights reserved. No part of this book may be reproduced or transmitted in any form or by any electronic or mechanical means, including photocopying, recording or by any information storage and retrieval system, without the express written permission of the copyright holder, except where permitted by law. This novel is a work of fiction. Names, characters, places and incidents are either the product of the author's imagination, or, if real, used fictitiously.

The ebook edition of this book is licensed for your personal enjoyment only. The ebook may not be re-sold or given away to other people. If you would like to share the ebook edition with another person, please purchase an additional copy for each recipient. Thank you for respecting the hard work of this author.

EBook ISBN: 978-1-68057-701-3
Trade Paperback ISBN: 978-1-68057-702-0
Dust Jacket Hardcover ISBN: 978-1-68057-703-7
Library of Congress Control Number: 2024937323
Cover design by Janet McDonald
Cover artwork images from Adobe Stock
Vellum layout by CJ Anaya
Kevin J. Anderson, Art Director
Published by
WordFire Press, LLC
PO Box 1840
Monument CO 80132
Kevin J. Anderson & Rebecca Moesta, Publishers
WordFire Press eBook Edition 2024
WordFire Press Trade Paperback Edition 2024
WordFire Press Dust Jacket Hardcover Edition 2024

Printed in the USA
Join our WordFire Press Readers Group for
sneak previews, updates, new projects, and giveaways.
Sign up at wordfirepress.com

*This is for Ray Bradbury—friend and mentor.
Thanks for giving me a huge book of poetry for my 14th birthday.
The New Oxford Book of English Verse, 1250–1950 had 974 pages of poems
covering seven hundred years and included works ranging from William
Allingham to W.B. Yeats. No single gift of a book has ever made as profound
an impact on me, and that is saying quite a lot. You unlocked a love of poetry
that grows stronger every single year. What a gift of immeasurable value.*

And, as always, for Sara Jo ...

Contents

Editor's Foreword	xiii
"A Corpse Going to a Ball" by Seba Smith *Selected and with Commentary by Tonya Hurley*	1
"A Man Said to the Universe" by Stephen Crane *Selected and with Commentary by Hailey Piper*	5
"A Musical Instrument" by Elizabeth Barrett Browning *Selected and with Commentary by Lisa Brackmann*	7
"A Pæan" by Edgar Allan Poe *Selected and with Commentary by Ray Garton*	10
"After Death" by Algernon Charles Swinburne *Selected and with Commentary by Greg Mollin*	14
"Alone" by Edgar Allan Poe *Selected and with Commentary by Jay Bonansinga*	18
"America a Prophecy" by William Blake *Selected and with Commentary by Keith R.A. DeCandido*	20
"Annabel Lee" by Edgar Allan Poe *Selected and with Commentary by Alma Katsu*	23
"Medusa's Tears" by Dr. Janina Scarlet *An Essay on Personal Darkness*	26
"Antigonish" by William Hughes Mearns *Selected and with Commentary by Jessica McHugh*	28
"Ah, Are You Digging on My Grave" by Thomas Hardy *Selected and with Commentary by Gregory Frost*	30
"Because I Could Not Stop for Death" by Emily Dickinson *Selected and with Commentary by Z Brewer*	33
"Bothwell's Bonny Jane" by Matthew G. Lewis *Selected and with Commentary by Lisa Morton*	36
"A Brown Girl Dead" by Countee Cullen *Selected and with Commentary by Lucy Snyder*	42
"The Waste Land: The Burial of the Dead" by T.S. Eliot *Selected and with Commentary by John Palisano*	44
"Canis Major" by Robert Frost *Selected and with Commentary by Alessandro Manzetti*	47
"Childe Roland to the Dark Tower Came" by Robert Browning *Selected and with Commentary by John Langan*	49
"Darkness" by George Gordon (Lord) Byron *Selected and with Commentary by Del Howison*	56

"Death Be Not Proud" by John Donne   60
Selected and with Commentary by Charisma Carpenter

"Dulce et Decorum Est" by Wilfred Owen   62
Selected and with Commentary by Duane Swierczynski

"Eldorado" by Edgar Allan Poe   64
Selected and with Commentary by David Fitzgerald

"Exile" by Winifred Welles   66
Selected and with Commentary by Marguerite Reed

"Full Fathom Five" by William Shakespeare   68
Selected and with Commentary by Greg Cox

"The Cremation of Sam McGee" by Robert W. Service   70
Selected and with Commentary by R.L. Stine

"To the Right Honourable William, Earl of Dartmouth" by Phillis Wheatley   74
Selected and with Commentary by Sumiko Saulson

"Hymn to Pan" by John Keats   77
Selected and with Commentary by Jeffrey J. Mariotte

"I died for Beauty" by Emily Dickinson   80
Selected and with Commentary by Jane Yolen

"I felt a Funeral, in my Brain" by Emily Dickinson   82
Selected and with Commentary by John Russo

"I Have a Dead Friend" by José Martí   85
Selected and with Commentary by Gaby Triana

"I Used to Be Invincible" by Weston Ochse   88
Selected and with Commentary by Yvonne Navarro

"If We Must Die" by Claude McKay   90
Selected and with Commentary by Harold Perrineau

"In Flanders Fields" by John McCrae   92
Selected and with Commentary by Charlaine Harris

"in Just" by e.e. cummings   94
Selected and with Commentary by Shane Black

"In the Desert" by Stephen Crane   96
Selected and with Commentary by Cullen Bunn

"Terror Management and the Worm at the Core" by Travis Langley   98
An Essay on Darkness

"Jessie Cameron" by Christina Rossetti   100
Selected and with Commentary by Dennis Tafoya

"On Joy and Sorrow" by Kahlil Gibran   105
Submitted and with Commentary by Lisa Diane Kastner

"Jubilate Agno" by Christopher Smart   107
Selected and with Commentary by Charlie Jane Anders

"La Belle Dame sans Merci" by John Keats   111
Selected and with Commentary by Melissa Marr

"Le Léthé" by Charles Baudelaire *Selected and with Commentary by Delilah S. Dawson*	114
"Mexican Poetry" by Jose de Saltillo *Selected and with Commentary by V. Castro*	116
"My Last Duchess" by Robert Browning *Selected and with Commentary by Stephen Graham Jones*	119
"Nathicana" by H.P. Lovecraft *Selected and with Commentary by Samantha Underhill*	122
"Nyarlathotep" by H.P. Lovecraft *Submitted and with Commentary by Isaac Marion*	126
"On Being Brought from Africa to America" by Phillis Wheatley *Selected and with Commentary by Tananarive Due*	130
"On Viewing the Skull and Bones of a Wolf" by Alexander Posey *Selected and with Commentary by Marsheila Rockwell*	132
"The Absence of Light" by Millicent San Juan, PsyD *An Essay on Darkness*	134
"One Need Not be a Chamber—to be Haunted" by Emily Dickinson *Selected and with Commentary by Jess Landry*	136
"Ozymandias" by Percy Bysshe Shelley *Selected and with Commentary by Bev Vincent*	138
"Poor Jack" by H.C. Dodge *Selected and with Commentary by Grady Hendrix*	140
"Porphyria's Lover" by Robert Browning *Selected and with Commentary by Brenna Yovanoff*	142
"Resumé" by Dorothy Parker *Selected and with Commentary by John Skipp*	145
"Richard Cory" by Edwin Arlington Robinson *Selected and with Commentary by Hallie Ephron*	147
"Rizpah" by Alfred Lord Tennyson *Selected and with Commentary by Ramsey Campbell*	149
"Sick Room" by Langston Hughes *Selected and with Commentary by Linda D. Addison*	155
"Spellbound" by Emily Brontë *Submitted and with Commentary by Christina Sng*	157
"Stagolee" by Author Unknown *Selected and with Commentary by Gary Phillips*	159
"Storm Fear" by Robert Frost *Selected with Commentary by Jezzy Wolfe*	161
"Suicide's Note" by Langston Hughes *Selected and with Commentary by Amber Benson*	163
"The City in the Sea" by Edgar Allan Poe *Selected and with Commentary by Kami Garcia*	165

"Ghost Road" by Lisa Fredsti — 168
Selected and with Commentary by Dana Fredsti

"Erlkönig" by Johann Wolfgang von Goethe — 171
Selected and with Commentary by Nancy Holder

"The Fairies" by William Allingham — 174
Selected and with Commentary by Jacopo della Quercia

"The Giaour" by George Gordon, Lord Byron — 177
Selected and with Commentary by Leslie S. Klinger

"The Grave of the Slave" by Sarah Louise Forten — 179
Selected and with Commentary by Victor LaValle

"The Highwayman" by Alfred Noyes — 181
Selected and with Commentary by Angela Yuriko Smith

"The Hollow Men" by T.S. Eliot — 186
Selected and with Commentary by James Aquilone

"The Lady of Shalott" by Alfred Lord Tennyson — 190
Selected and with Commentary by Paul Cornell

"The Little Ghost" by Edna St. Vincent Millay — 197
Selected and with Commentary by Stephanie M. Wytovich

"The March of the Dead" by Robert Service — 199
Selected and with Commentary by Christopher Golden

"The Mermaid" by William Butler Yeats — 203
Selected and with Commentary by Laurell K. Hamilton

"The Only Ghost I Ever Saw" by Emily Dickinson — 205
Selected and with Commentary by Anne Walsh

"The Opal Dream Cave" by Katherine Mansfield — 207
Selected and with Commentary by Lee Murray

Editor's Note — 210

"The Raven" by Edgar Allan Poe — 211
Selected and with Commentary by Eileen M. D'Angelo

"The Raven" by Edgar Allan Poe — 217
Selected and with Commentary by Scott Brick

"The Ruined Chapel" by William Allingham — 219
Selected and with Commentary by Tim Lebbon

"The Second Coming" by W.B. Yeats — 221
Selected and with Commentary by Craig Engler

"Laughter's Dark Side" by Travis Adams — 223
A Brief Essay

"The Shadow on the Stone" by Thomas Hardy — 225
Selected and with Commentary by Ray Porter

"The Shipwrecked Sailor" By Ameni-amenaa — 227
Selected and with Commentary by David Wellington

"The Sleeper" by Edgar Allan Poe — 230
Selected and with Commentary by Joe R. Lansdale

"The Spider and the Fly" by Mary Howitt — 233
Selected and with Commentary by Scott Sigler

"The Twa Corbies" by Author Unknown 236
Selected and with Commentary by Seanan McGuire

"The Witch" by Mary Elizabeth Coleridge 238
Selected and with Commentary by Rio Youers

"The Witches Spell" by William Shakespeare 240
Selected and with Commentary by Simon Vance

"The Yuki-Onna" by Lafcadio Hearn 243
Selected and with Commentary by Kevin Wetmore

"They Flee from Me" by Sir Thomas Wyatt 246
Selected and with Commentary by Mary A. Turzillo

"This Living Hand" by John Keats 248
Submitted and with Commentary by Marge Simon

"To——. Ulalume: A Ballad" by Edgar Allan Poe 250
Selected and with Commentary by Josh Malerman

"Tomino's Hell" by Saijō Yaso 254
Selected and with Commentary by Jamie Ford

"Waltzing Matilda" by Andrew Barton "Banjo" Paterson 256
Selected and with Commentary by Robbie Coburn

"We Wear the Mask" Paul Laurence Dunbar 259
Selected and with Commentary by Maurice Broaddus

"We Will All Go Together When We Go" by Tom Lehrer 261
Selected and with Commentary by Linda Nagle

"What the Moon Brings" by H.P. Lovecraft 264
Selected and with Commentary by Maxwell I. Gold

"The Stolen Child" by William Butler Yeats 267
Selected and with Commentary by Jonathan Maberry

Acknowledgments 271
About the Editor 273

Editor's Foreword
Darkness Calls with Many Voices

I have a strange and dark history with poetry.
    It is not a stretch to say that poetry saved my life. Likely more than once. My introduction to it, though, was joyful.
    When I was in seventh grade, the librarian at my middle school—a wonderful woman named Abigail Smith—became a mentor. This was a school in an economically depressed section of inner-city Philadelphia. Everyone's fathers had been in World War II or Korea. Everyone's brothers and uncles were going to Vietnam. Most of the kids in my neighborhood had three possible career paths—they could enlist when they were old enough and let the military educate them, they could try for a sports scholarship somewhere, or they could do what their parents did and go work in one of the many factories that surrounded our tiny row homes.
    I didn't want to do any of those things. I wanted to be a writer. I was already an obsessive reader, having discovered Robert E. Howard, Ed McBain, Michael Moorcock, Louis L'Amour, and Edgar Rice Burroughs. I was one of the *only* kids in my school who voluntarily went into the library. Not to get something for required reading, but because I wanted to find stuff I wanted to read. Adventures, science fiction, fantasy.
    Miss Smith, however, had an interesting policy. Maybe she shared it with others, I don't actually know. Her thing was that if someone came into her domain to get something they wanted, she provided it but *heavily* encouraged them to check out something else that was not in their preferred comfort zone.
    I got the full treatment because I was a regular in that palace of books. I'd go in for a Tarzan or action western and come out with one of those and maybe a contemporary novel, maybe romance, maybe historical fiction, maybe nonfiction. That was the rhythm.

That alone would have made her my hero because my father—who was not a good person by any metric—did not allow me to have books. He felt all of my reading was my attempt to "get above myself." Arguments were shortcuts to beatings, so I began hiding my books at my grandmother's house or leaving them with friends.

The second thing that made her remarkable was that she was the secretary for two different clubs of professional writers. One was a science-fiction and heroic fantasy group called The Hyborian Legion, and it met in Philadelphia. The meetings were usually at the home of author, editor, curmudgeon George Scithers. One of the regulars was L. Sprague de Camp—a fact that astounded me because the very first book I ever bought with my own money was *Conan the Wanderer*, a collection of sword-and-sorcery stories he and Lin Carter had done—completing some of Robert E. Howard's unfinished tales and revising others of Howard's adventure stories to become Conan tales.

De Camp was a superhero to me, and we became friends as I grew older, and remained friends all the way to his death in 2000. It was de Camp who later introduced me to H.P. Lovecraft and many others who wrote for *Weird Tales Magazine*. I now edit that magazine, so there is a longer legacy story in that, but this isn't the time for it.

The second group in which Miss Smith was involved was a kind of ongoing cocktail party at a publisher's penthouse in New York. This was 1970, and if you were an author of note, you went to New York to launch your books. When there was enough critical mass of genre writers in town, the publisher had a party. Miss Smith would go up and act as hostess and—given how many writers are moody and taciturn—conversation facilitator. She got my grandmother to forge my father's signature so I could come along. God only knows where my father thought I was actually going. Nor did he appear to care.

The very first of those events I attended in New York while still a scruffy twelve-year-old had a guest list that would change the course of my life. Ray Bradbury, Richard Matheson, Avram Davidson, Robert Bloch, and Harlan Ellison were all there.

I had no idea who most of them were, and zero idea who Bradbury was. I asked him if he was a writer and if he'd ever been published. You can imagine the tear-streaming, gut-busting hilarity that ensued from the other writers. Ray, though, was amused and kind and explained that, yes, he had taken a swing at writing a time or two.

Once all of the dreadful embarrassment was past, Bradbury and Matheson began to grill me. Miss Smith had told them I wanted to be a writer, and I guess those two literary giants determined that maybe I would be. They told me about writing, about publishing, and about what mattered to them in terms of literature.

Bradbury asked me what I liked to read. I said that I liked "dark stuff."

They asked why. Specifically, Matheson asked if I liked monsters. I thought about it and said, no ... I like people who fight monsters.

It was a revelation to me as well, though with time's perspective I know that I was talking about my home life. My father was a brutal man. Abusive, caustic, belittling, violent. He cast a dark pall over my young life and the lives of my sisters. It was like living in a troll cave. It was like being trapped in Dracula's basement.

The second time I met Bradbury, he gave me a shopping bag full of books. Not sure if Miss Smith had told him that I was very poor and that it took me weeks of doing odd jobs to even buy that copy of *Conan the Wanderer*, and it was a Lancer paperback with a sixty-cent price. Yes, we were that poor.

The bag of books Bradbury gave me included several of his, some of Matheson's (who later brought a bag of books for me, too), and works by writers I'd never heard of. Alexandre Dumas, John D. MacDonald, H.G. Wells, Jules Verne, Edgar Allan Poe, and others.

And at the bottom of the bag was a very thick hardcover, *The New Oxford Book of English Verse 1250–1950*—which I mentioned in this volume's dedication. Nearly one thousand pages of poetry.

Until then, the only poems I'd ever heard were Christmas carols, lyrics in liner notes of my older sisters' rock'n'roll albums, and "The Raven" by Poe, which had been read by one of my teachers in sixth grade during a Halloween event. I was not a fan of poetry because, up until then, I hadn't really read it.

"What's so big about this stuff?" I asked.

Instead of a rebuke, Bradbury sat me down in a corner and began telling me *about* poetry. He explained how poets possess an enviable talent for brevity. He, of course, had to explain brevity and its value, but he made his point. He said, "A poet can take the most complex emotion and distill it down to a few lines that often tells us more than a whole chapter of prose. And it does so in a way that invites the reader to help conjure the images and grasp the concepts." He went on—then and at other times—to school me on the basics of imagery and allegory, metaphor and hyperbole, and lots of other aspects of language, assuring me that if I wanted to be a good writer of short stories and novels, then I should become a student of poetry.

He also gave me one of his "rules for a good life," and that was "Always know more than you're taught." He said poetry encourages thought more so than mere reaction. I think that was the first really deep thing I ever understood.

And he told me that poetry was a candle to hold against the darkness.

We were to have many conversations about darkness. About what it is, about its chameleon nature, about its horrors and its beauty. About the many kinds of darkness.

For most kids, darkness was whatever was under the bed or in the closet.

For my sisters and I, the monster wasn't under the bed, he lived in the bedroom down the hall. Not far enough down the hall. Our home was dark, and our father thrived in those shadows.

I had never discussed my father's abusive nature with Miss Smith, but I know for certain that she saw the marks darkness had left on me. And that does not mean the bruises, the limps, the tendency to flinch.

I don't know this for certain, but I think she had a conversation about this with Ray Bradbury. Maybe with Harlan Ellison and Richard Matheson too. They often brought me books about people who confronted darkness. *Dracula, Heart of Darkness, To Kill a Mockingbird, I Am Legend* ... countless others.

Of all the books they gave me, it was Bradbury's gift of that poetry book that did the most for me. I took it home and lied to my father that it was a schoolbook. Required reading. He merely sneered at it and let me have it.

How many nights did I crouch under a blanket with a flashlight reading the poetry of Matthew Arnold, William Blake, John Keats, Dylan Thomas, William Wordsworth, Alfred Lord Tennyson, Lord Byron, Percy Shelley ...

So many.

And so many poems about death and loss, about dying in war, about desolation, about grief and trauma.

Poems in which some of the greatest poets in history explored darkness. Oh, sure, not all poems were dark, but enough were.

It is a strange phenomenon when an abused and terrified child realizes that he is not alone. Yes, it sounds odd to suggest that one abused person can take comfort in the knowledge that others have suffered similarly. No, that's not unkindness. Rather the reverse, it's where empathy is born. Empathy being far more powerful a force than sympathy.

I read and reread those poems. I gravitated to Poe—partly because he wrote great spooky stories, but mainly because he wrote about his losses, his grief. I found some of this examined in other ways by Byron and Donne and others. William Ernest Henley's "Invictus" was life-changing for me. As was T.S. Eliot's "The Waste Land," which was to me not a poem about World War I, as one review I read insisted. For me it was a way of understanding the shadows and darkness I saw in my older brother when he came home from Vietnam, surrounded by the ghosts of his friends and his innocence.

This volume of verse is the result of more than five decades of brooding on the nature of darkness as expressed in poetry. Because I'm mostly known as a writer of horror and dark fantasy, some might assume this is a collection of horror poetry. It's not, although there are horror poems herein. Nor is it a book whose focus is negativity, because it's not that either. Darkness—like order and chaos—is neither absolutely good nor bad. It is whatever we decide it is.

The child I had been was afraid of the darkness of night because that's when my father's predatory nature was rampant. Yet at the same time, darkness was somewhere to hide. It was a shelter. And the darkness of my angry, hurt, furious childhood thoughts were pressure valves, allowing me to imagine bad things—mostly directed at my father—without ever having to take actions in the shape of revenge. For a lot of my peers who write creepy stuff, we do it because some kinds of darkness are better out than in, and reading is as cathartic as writing.

For some—and often for me—darkness is beautiful. The world becomes visually simpler, and yet the certain knowledge that things are awake and alive in the night is quite enchanting. There is darkness in space, where my mind often wanders. There is darkness in caves, where some people go exploring in search of excitement, grandeur, and understanding.

There is the darkness of grief. Yes. In fact, one of the poems in this book, "I Used to be Invincible," was written by a dear friend as he lay dying; and the commentary was written by his wife and widow.

There is the darkness of cultural atrocity, as reflected in some poems about race and abuse. There is darkness about the larger world that we don't understand. There is darkness in loss and trauma and personal damage.

And yet ... in none of these cases is *darkness* the point. It is a place we can go in the quietness of our hearts and minds to understand, to process, to gain perspective, to heal, to learn, to share. The darkness shared by the many creatives in this book is there to begin conversations and stoke the fires of introspection.

Darkness speaks to us in so many voices.

I created this anthology because of my love of poetry, my appreciation for the many facets of darkness, and to do some good. None of us are paid for our work in this book. All of the proceeds will go toward sponsorships and other charitable works associated with Superstars Writing Seminars, a conference founded to help emerging writers learn the aspects of business that will help them bring their voices and their writings into the light.

All of the folks I asked to be involved—and it's an astounding lineup—agreed without question to do this. To write commentary on classic poems that speak of darkness. To share their insights, and many are quite personal and confessional. There are also four short essays in which mental health professionals discuss the nature of darkness.

There are long and short poems, prose poems, song lyrics, ballads, and different styles of verse, and more. There are even two sets of commentary on one poem (Poe's "The Raven") as a way of illustrating how the same poem lends itself to endless interpretation. Some of these poems you've likely seen and read before, perhaps in school. Others are far more obscure and will therefore be new to most readers. There are close to a hundred poems, and no two approach darkness in the same way or for the same reason. That's a kind of magic, and it's in here.

I hope you find within these pages poems that speak to your heart, that open your mind, and which offer good company no matter how deep the darkness.

Thank you for buying this book and for the good it will do.

Darkness does indeed speak with many voices. And I encourage you to pause ... and to listen.

—Jonathan Maberry
2024, San Diego, CA

"A Corpse Going to a Ball"
by Seba Smith
Selected and with Commentary
by Tonya Hurley

Young Charlotte lived by the mountainside,
A wild and lonely spot;
No dwelling there, for three miles round,
Except her father's cot;

And yet on many a winter's eve
Young swains were gather'd there,
For her father kept a social board,
And she was very fair.

Her father loved to see her dress'd
As prim as a city belle,
For she was all the child he had,
And he loved his daughter well.

'Tis New Year's eve — the sun is down —
Why looks her restless eye
So long from the frosty window forth,
As the merry sleighs go by?

At the village inn, fifteen miles off,
Is a merry ball to-night —
The piercing air is cold as death,
But her heart is warm and light;

And brightly beams her laughing eye,
As a well-known voice she hears;

And dashing up to the cottage door
Her Charley's sleigh appears.

"Now daughter dear," her mother cried,
"This blanket round you fold,
"For 'tis a dreadful night abroad,
"You'll catch your death a-cold."

"O nay, O nay," fair Charlotte said,
And she laugh'd like a gypsy queen,
"To ride with blankets muffled up
"I never could be seen—

"My silken cloak is quite enough;
"You know 'tis lined throughout;
"And then I have a silken shawl
"To tie my neck about."

Her bonnet and her gloves are on,
She jumps into the sleigh;
And swift they ride by the mountainside,
And over the hills away.

There's life in the sound of the merry bells,
As over the hills they go;
But a creaking wail the runners make,
As they bite the frozen snow.

How long the bleak and lonely way!
How keen the wind does blow!
The stars did never shine so cold—
How creaks the frozen snow!

With muffled faces, silently,
Five cold, long miles they've pass'd,
And Charles, with these few frozen words,
The silence broke at last—

"Such night as this I never saw—
"The reins I scarce can hold;"
And Charlotte, shivering, faintly said,
"I am exceeding cold."

He crack'd his whip, and urged his steed
More swiftly than before,

And now five other dreary miles
In silence are pass'd o'er—

"How fast," said Charles "the freezing ice"
"Is gathering on my brow;"
But Charlotte said, with feebler lone.
"I'm growing warmer now."

And on they went through the frosty air
And the glittering, cold star-light;
And now at last the village inn
And the ball-room are in sight.

They reach the door, and Charles jumps out,
And holds his hand to her—
Why sits she like a monument,
That hath no power to stir

He call'd her once—he call'd her twice—
She answer'd not a word;
He ask'd her for her hand again,
But still she never stirr'd—

He took her hand in his—O God!
'Twas cold and hard as stone;
He tore the mantle from her face;
The cold stars on her shone—

Then quickly to the lighted hall
Her voiceless form he bore—
His Charlotte was a stiffen'd corpse,
And word spake never more!

OBSERVATIONS

This poem was inspired by the story of Fair Charlotte, or Frozen Charlotte as she eventually came to be known. A cautionary tale about vanity and disobedience, the origin of Charlotte's story is found in an 18th-century article in the *New York Observer*, which, like all the best stories, may or may not have been true. Charlotte is warned by her mother to cover up for the long sleigh ride on a freezing New Year's Eve night on her way to the Ball, but she resists, preferring to have her lovely gown visible for all the world to see. She arrives at the dance dead and frozen over, "a stiffened corpse" as the poet Seba Smith so vividly describes her. Charlotte was neither the first nor the last young woman to sacrifice herself for fashion.

Yet her death, tragic as it is, is almost beside the point. There is something very modern about Charlotte and this chilling story that caught the public's imagination back then and remains strangely prophetic in the age of social media, product placement, fake news, and pop cultural fame. The *Observer* article went "viral" almost immediately, inspiring the poem, a popular folk ballad, a dessert, and, soon after, a Victorian-era preoccupation with white porcelain "penny dolls"—thought to match the dead girl's ghostly pallor. Exchanged among and collected by young girls, they came to be known as Frozen Charlottes.

A tradition of placing the dolls in tiny coffins, or even burying them once a child had grown tired of playthings, grew well into the early 20th century. For the boys there were Frozen Charlies, giving the poem and the legend a wider acceptance and even some, as we might call it today, Kenergy. Charlottes and Charlies still pop up from their resting places from time to time in museums and thrift shops around the world. The story succeeds not only as literature but as a rudimentary and effective kind of branding. Just to close this past-its prologue loop, I confess that I collect and sold these dolls at our Morbid Anatomy Museum and that "A Corpse Going to a Ball" was the impetus for my own *ghostgirl* book series (Little, Brown), inspiring the name of the main character, who also lost her life trying to get to the big dance.

About Tonya Hurley

Tonya Hurley is a *New York Times* and international bestselling author of the *ghostgirl* series and the Blessed trilogy, and a screenwriter. Her books are published in nearly thirty countries, in more than twenty languages around the world, and have received starred reviews from such literary publications as *Publishers Weekly*, *Voice of Youth Advocates* magazine, the *School Library Journal*, and *Kirkus Reviews*. She wrote and produced two hit TV series and wrote and directed several acclaimed independent films—which have premiered in film festivals around the world and are broadcast on such outlets as PBS and IFC. Hurley is a founding board member of the Morbid Anatomy Museum and now runs Hurley Sister's Productions for film and TV.

"A Man Said to the Universe" by Stephen Crane

Selected and with Commentary by Hailey Piper

A man said to the universe:
"Sir, I exist!"
"However," replied the universe,
"The fact has not created in me
A sense of obligation."

Observations

I first encountered Stephen Crane's "A Man Said to the Universe" in high school—I forget which year's English class—as a quick way to prime teenagers for the concept of existentialism before we began reading *The Stranger* by Albert Camus. Being a depressed teen, I had mixed feelings, but the poem never left me. In time, I began to recognize its themes as part of a particular horror subgenre—cosmic horror.

Those final words ring through me: "A sense of obligation." Cosmic horror often involves forces of such grandiose scale that humanity seems insignificant. This can mean unthinking elements, such as the cold of space battering our world with no obligation to care who exists here. But cosmic horror is a vast subgenre, and a lack of a sense of obligation is up for interpretation. There's no obligation to recognition, but also no obligation to kindness. A universe can contain malice. The lack of obligation to a person's existence can mean a desire to erase that existence. To make it *not* a fact. And really, nonexistence strikes every day. People keep declaring they exist, through song, art, connections, conversation, pretend rules they slap onto the world, and yet they keep ending. We crawl across the surface of a world, and the planets spin, and they revolve around their stars, and the galaxy swirls with billions of stars among billions of galaxies, and on a universal scale, millions of years after a death, it might not even have noticed that it hates us.

But whether apathy or malice, I think there's also a contrarianism in my work against the poem too. Always aware of it, mindful of the potential reaction "oh no, mankind is not important on a universal scale." Except we don't live on a universal scale, so who cares? The universe might not create in others a sense of obligation either. See, apathy works both ways. All that celestial movement and indifference and potential for hateful forces, and yet we keep declaring we exist. And even when one of us ends, universe be damned, more of us have only just begun.

About Hailey Piper

Hailey Piper is the Bram Stoker Award-winning author of Queen of Teeth. Her other works include A Light Most Hateful, the Worm and His Kings series, and other books of dark fiction. She is an active member of the Horror Writers Association, with over one hundred short stories appearing in Weird Tales, Pseudopod, Cosmic Horror Monthly, and other publications. Her nonfiction appears in Writer's Digest, Library Journal, CrimeReads, and elsewhere. She lives with her wife in Maryland, where their cosmic rituals are secret. Find Hailey at haileypiper.com.

"A Musical Instrument"
by Elizabeth Barrett Browning
Selected and with Commentary
by Lisa Brackmann

I.
WHAT was he doing, the great god Pan,
Down in the reeds by the river?
Spreading ruin and scattering ban,
Splashing and paddling with hoofs of a goat,
And breaking the golden lilies afloat
With the dragon-fly on the river.

II.
He tore out a reed, the great god Pan,
From the deep cool bed of the river:
The limpid water turbidly ran,
And the broken lilies a-dying lay,
And the dragon-fly had fled away,
Ere he brought it out of the river.

III.
High on the shore sate the great god Pan,
While turbidly flowed the river;
And hacked and hewed as a great god can,
With his hard bleak steel at the patient reed,
Till there was not a sign of a leaf indeed
To prove it fresh from the river.

IV.
He cut it short, did the great god Pan,
(How tall it stood in the river!)

Then drew the pith, like the heart of a man,
Steadily from the outside ring,
And notched the poor dry empty thing
In holes, as he sate by the river.

V.
'This is the way,' laughed the great god Pan,
(Laughed while he sate by the river,)
'The only way, since gods began
To make sweet music, they could succeed.'
Then, dropping his mouth to a hole in the reed,
He blew in power by the river.

VI.
Sweet, sweet, sweet, O Pan!
Piercing sweet by the river!
Blinding sweet, O great god Pan!
The sun on the hill forgot to die,
And the lilies revived, and the dragon-fly
Came back to dream on the river.

VII.
Yet half a beast is the great god Pan,
To laugh as he sits by the river,
Making a poet out of a man:
The true gods sigh for the cost and pain,—
For the reed which grows nevermore again
As a reed with the reeds in the river.

Observations

I hope you'll bear with me. When I was first asked if I wanted to contribute to this wonderful collection, I thought, "Cool! I'll talk about Yeats's "The Second Coming," one of my very favorite poems of all times!" It is also at least one other contributor's favorite, so I needed to make another choice. Apparently, I share tastes with a few contributors to this anthology, because my second and third choices were taken as well. That exhausted my poetry knowledge bank, so I had to do some research.

Which brings me to "A Musical Instrument," by Elizabeth Barrett Browning.

Elizabeth Barrett Browning was famous in her day, and not just lady famous—she was one of the most popular poets of the Victorian era.

"How do I love thee? Let me count the ways."

That's Elizabeth Barrett Browning.

She was also a supporter of Mary Wollstonecraft's political ideas, an abolitionist from a Jamaican slaveholder family, and a chronically ill woman dependent on opiates to treat severe pain from an illness that physicians of the time were unable to diagnose. She married another famous Victorian poet, Robert Browning, and they spent most of their life together in Florence, Italy. Their circle of associates included well-known artists and writers like George Sand, Harriet Beecher Stowe, and Alfred Tennyson. In her lifetime, she was popular and respected, and when she died at the age of fifty-five, she was widely mourned.

When I first read "A Musical Instrument," I was puzzled. All of this drama over pulling out a reed! But there was no denying the disturbing, violent undertones of the imagery: The hacking and hewing, the drawing of the pith, "like the heart of a man," the ruthless shaping of the reed to become an instrument of Pan's own power, one that made music so beautiful that the implied violence of the previous stanzas is all but forgotten. The narrator has not forgotten, though, as "The true gods sigh for the cost and the pain" of a reed cut down and forced into a form that diminishes it and sucks it dry, even if it does become the core of Pan's famous panpipes.

It turns out that Barrett Browning based her poem on a specific Greek myth, that of Pan and the wood nymph Syrinx. Syrinx was a follower of Artemis, the Huntress, and though she had vowed to remain a virgin, that meant nothing to Pan, who wanted Syrinx for his own. The Naiads of the river transformed Syrinx into a bundle of reeds in a vain attempt to help her escape Pan. Since he could not have her as a woman, Pan cut her down as a reed and shaped her to his liking, took her pith and her heart for his own music.

A lot of women know what that particular horror is like.

"A Musical Instrument" was Elizabeth Barrett Browning's final poem, published posthumously.

About Lisa Brackmann

Lisa Brackmann is *The New York Times* bestselling author of the Ellie McEnroe trilogy (*Rock Paper Tiger, Hour of the Rat, Dragon Day*), and suspense novels *Getaway, Go-Between*, and *Black Swan Rising*. When she isn't writing, she's playing bass guitar, rooting for the San Diego Padres from her home in Humboldt County, and servicing every need of her two demanding cats.

"A Pæan" by Edgar Allan Poe
Selected and with Commentary by Ray Garton

I.
How shall the burial rite be read?
The solemn song be sung?
The requiem for the loveliest dead,
That ever died so young?

II.
Her friends are gazing on her,
And on her gaudy bier,
And weep!—oh! to dishonor
Dead beauty with a tear!

III.
They loved her for her wealth—
And they hated her for her pride—
But she grew in feeble health,
And they *love* her—that she died.

IV.
They tell me (while they speak
Of her "costly broider'd pall")
That my voice is growing weak—
That I should not sing at all—

V.
Or that my tone should be
Tun'd to such solemn song

So mournfully—so mournfully,
That the dead may feel no wrong.

VI.
But she is gone above,
With young Hope at her side,
And I am drunk with love
Of the dead, who is my bride.—

VII.
Of the dead—dead who lies
All perfum'd there,
With the death upon her eyes,
And the life upon her hair.

VIII.
Thus on the coffin loud and long
I strike—the murmur sent
Through the grey chambers to my song,
Shall be the accompaniment.

IX.
Thou died'st in thy life's June—
But thou did'st not die too fair:
Thou did'st not die too soon,
Nor with too calm an air.

X.
From more than fiends on earth,
Thy life and love are riven,
To join the untainted mirth
Of more than thrones in heaven—

XII.
Therefore, to thee this night
I will no requiem raise,
But waft thee on thy flight,
With a Pæan of old days.

OBSERVATIONS

I must admit, I'm not much of a reader of poetry, but I do enjoy the brooding, lyrical, and evocative poems of Edgar Allan Poe. I first became familiar with "A Pæan" when I was searching for a title for a novel I was writing, a ghost story. My longtime agent and friend, Richard Curtis, directed me to something in this poem. It was in the first stanza:
How shall the burial rite be read?
The solemn song be sung?
The requiem for the loveliest dead,
That ever died so young?
The novel became *The Loveliest Dead*. But the poem stayed with me. I think it stands out among Poe's poems. In spite of the dark setting and bleakness of the subject, Poe decides to let in some light. Instead of singing a pæan to his dead love, instead of dwelling on the fact that she is dead and clinging to the sadness that goes with that, he decides to sing a joyous recognition of the life she led. That's a departure from the intense darkness that inhabits so much of his fiction and poetry. It contains a note of human hope.

Let me explain what I mean by "human hope." We human beings are geared to see the worst thing in the room. Our attention automatically goes to the most threatening thing in our vicinity, which often kicks in the fight-or-flight response. That was an ability we developed very early in the life of our species, a way to protect us, to feed us. We brought it out of the wilderness with us when we set up this whole civilization thing, and it has caused no end of havoc among humans ever since. It's something we all struggle with, this eye for trouble, this propensity to focus on the negative, and when not properly managed, it can make us kind of paranoid, or just plain crazy. To deal with it, we must resist it at times—most times!—and here in this poem we see Poe doing precisely that. He makes the conscious choice—because that's what it takes, making a conscious choice not to follow the orders of our wiring—to celebrate rather than mourn, to sing rather than cry. I think it's a beautiful poem.

About Ray Garton

Ray Garton is the author of a number of celebrated books, mostly in the horror genre, including his Frankenstorm series and the wildly popular *Live Girls*. He writes for adults and young adults (as Joseph Locke). His short works are collected into *Methods of Madness and Pieces of Hate*. He's also written media tie-in fiction, including *Invaders from Mars*, *A Nightmare on Elm Street 4: The Dream Master*, *A Nightmare on Elm Street 5: The Dream Child*, and *Sabrina, the Teenage Witch: All that Glitters*. He was honored with the World Convention Grand Master Award at the World

Horror Convention in San Francisco. Find him online at raygartononline.com.

"After Death"
by Algernon Charles Swinburne
Selected and with Commentary
by Greg Mollin

The four boards of the coffin lid
Heard all the dead man did.

The first curse was in his mouth,
Made of grave's mould and deadly drouth.

The next curse was in his head,
Made of God's work discomfited.

The next curse was in his hands,
Made out of two grave-bands.

The next curse was in his feet,
Made out of a grave-sheet.

"I had fair coins red and white,
And my name was as great light;

I had fair clothes green and red,
And strong gold bound round my head.

But no meat comes in my mouth,
Now I fare as the worm doth;

And no gold binds in my hair,
Now I fare as the blind fare.

My live thews were of great strength,
Now am I waxen a span's length;

My live sides were full of lust,
Now are they dried with dust."

The first board spake and said:
"Is it best eating flesh or bread?"

The second answered it:
"Is wine or honey the more sweet?"

The third board spake and said:
"Is red gold worth a girl's gold head?"

The fourth made answer thus:
"All these things are as one with us."

The dead man asked of them:
"Is the green land stained brown with flame?

Have they hewn my son for beasts to eat,
And my wife's body for beasts' meat?

Have they boiled my maid in a brass pan,
And built a gallows to hang my man?"

The boards said to him:
"This is a lewd thing that ye deem.

Your wife has gotten a golden bed,
All the sheets are sewn with red.

Your son has gotten a coat of silk,
The sleeves are soft as curded milk.

Your maid has gotten a kirtle new,
All the skirt has braids of blue.

Your man has gotten both ring and glove,
Wrought well for eyes to love."

The dead man answered thus:
"What good gift shall God give us?"

The boards answered him anon:
"Flesh to feed hell's worm upon."

OBSERVATIONS

I was first introduced to the poetry of Swinburne in fifth grade, shortly after discovering the works of Edgar Allan Poe. I had memorized Poe's "Spirits of the Dead" for an English assignment, and my teacher, Mr. Williams, hip to my growing interest in darker poetry and literature, told me about another kindred poet named Algernon Charles Swinburne who was known as a writer of taboo and risqué subjects. I was intrigued. Much like Poe, even Swinburne's name had an enigmatic ring to it.

I hunted down a copy of *Poems and Ballads* at my local library and was delighted to discover they tread some similar ground in tone and subject. There were incredible poems of love and loss and plenty of themes I was too young and ignorant to grasp at that age, but there were also many poems of death and tragedy, which I found very captivating at the time. There was an underlying sense of irony in a lot of the work, and a sarcastic, anti-theistic tone that spoke to me almost as much as the darker imagery. The poem "After Death" encompassed all of those ideas and became an immediate and lasting favorite.

In "After Death" the narrator, dead and buried, speaks to the four walls of his coffin, reminiscing about his life and lamenting his demise. He worries over those he has left behind and is comforted to find that life continues on very well for his loved ones after his passing. Ultimately, he asks what sort of divine reward God has in store for him after death. The outlook for him, unfortunately, is not so wonderful.

One of my great joys as a bookseller is introducing customers to writers and poets that might be off their radar. Algernon Charles Swinburne is one that I frequently recommend to customers interested in Poe, Hawthorne, Lovecraft, and other writers of Gothic or dark Romanticism. H.P. Lovecraft called Swinburne "the only real poet in either England or America after the great Edgar Allan Poe." While I may not completely agree with that statement, I do still love his work and try to always have a collection of Swinburne's poetry on the shelves at Artifact Books and point out "After Death" as a favorite selection.

About Greg Mollin

Greg Mollin is a fiction writer and the owner/bookseller at Artifact Books, an independent bookstore in Encinitas, California. His stories have appeared in various print and digital publications, including *Weird Tales Magazine*; *Dark Moon Digest*; *Crime Factory Magazine*; *Thrillers, Killers, 'n' Chillers*; and *Burial Day Books*. Find him at artifactrarebooks.com and gregmollin.com.

"Alone" by Edgar Allan Poe
Selected and with Commentary by Jay Bonansinga

From childhood's hour I have not been
As others were—I have not seen
As others saw—I could not bring
My passions from a common spring—

From the same source I have not taken
My sorrow—I could not awaken
My heart to joy at the same tone—
And all I lov'd—*I* lov'd alone—

Then—in my childhood—in the dawn
Of a most stormy life—was drawn
From ev'ry depth of good and ill
The mystery which binds me still—

From the torrent, or the fountain—
From the red cliff of the mountain—
From the sun that 'round me roll'd
In its autumn tint of gold—

From the lightning in the sky
As it pass'd me flying by—
From the thunder, and the storm—
And the cloud that took the form
(When the rest of Heaven was blue)
Of a demon in my view.

Observations

I first encountered the poem "Alone" when I was twenty years old. Flirting with the prospects of becoming a professional writer, I had no idea that the author of this beautiful, sad, evocative poem had composed it when he was a mere twenty years old himself. I had no clue that this was a nerdy hipster from the 19th century reaching across time to inspire a nerdy hipster from the 20th (at the time enrolled in creative writing workshops at Michigan State University). I, who felt these same feelings, was oblivious to the fact that being an outsider is not only imperative to being a serious writer ... it's an almost universal condition of the young. It is also, in the hands of Edgar Allan Poe, a heartbreaking, haunting, eerie meditation on being human.

About Jay Bonansinga

Jay Bonansinga is *The New York Times*-bestselling author currently at work on a new series of superhero novels titled *Stan Lee's The Devil's Quartet* from TOR books. Jay is also the author of the blockbuster Walking Dead novels, in collaboration with the creator of the Walking Dead comics and TV series, Robert Kirkman. Additionally, Jay has authored over fifty acclaimed short stories and fifteen original novels, including the Bram Stoker finalist *The Black Mariah* (1994), the International Thriller Writers Award finalist *Shattered* (2007), and the acclaimed horror opus, *Self Storage* (2016). Jay's work has been translated into seventeen languages, and he has been called "one of the most imaginative writers of thrillers" by the *Chicago Tribune*. Jay's nonfiction work, *The Sinking of the Eastland* (2004), received national acclaim and ultimately became the source for the hit musical, *Eastland*, staged in Chicago by the Tony Award-winning theater company, Lookingglass. Jay's work as a screenwriter and film director has garnered him Best-of-Festival awards at the Houston, Queens, and Iowa City International film festivals. Jay also teaches creative writing at Northwestern University's School of Radio, Television & Film as well as the DePaul University's graduate English department.

"America a Prophecy"
by William Blake
Selected and with Commentary
by Keith R.A. DeCandido

(An excerpt of a longer work)

Sound! sound! my loud war-trumpets, and alarm my
    Thirteen Angels!
Loud howls the Eternal Wolf! the Eternal Lion lashes his
    tail!
America is dark'ned; and my punishing Demons, terrifièd,
Crouch howling before their caverns deep, like skins dry'd
    in the wind.
They cannot smite the wheat, nor quench the fatness of the
    earth;
They cannot smite with sorrows, nor subdue the plough
    and spade;
They cannot wall the city, nor moat round the castle of
    princes;
They cannot bring the stubbèd oak to overgrow the hills;
For terrible men stand on the shores, and in their robes I see
Children take shelter from the lightnings: there stands
    Washington,
And Paine, and Warren, with their foreheads rear'd toward
    the East
But clouds obscure my agèd sight. A vision from afar!
Sound! sound! my loud war-trumpets, and alarm my
    Thirteen Angels!
Ah, vision from afar! Ah, rebel form that rent the ancient
Heavens! Eternal Viper self-renew'd, rolling in clouds,
I see thee in thick clouds and darkness on America's shore,

Writhing in pangs of abhorrèd birth; red flames the crest rebellious
And eyes of death; the harlot womb, oft openèd in vain,
Heaves in enormous circles: now the times are return'd upon thee,
Devourer of thy parent, now thy unutterable torment renews.
Sound! sound! my loud war-trumpets, and alarm my Thirteen Angels!
Ah, terrible birth! a young one bursting! Where is the weeping mouth,
And where the mother's milk? Instead, those ever-hissing jaws
And parchèd lips drop with fresh gore: now roll thou in the clouds;
Thy mother lays her length outstretch'd upon the shore beneath.
Sound! sound! my loud war-trumpets, and alarm my Thirteen Angels!
Loud howls the Eternal Wolf! the Eternal Lion lashes his tail!
Thus wept the Angel voice, and as he wept the terrible blasts
Of trumpets blew a loud alarm across the Atlantic deep.
No trumpets answer; no reply of clarions or of fifes:
Silent the Colonies remain and refuse the loud alarm.
On those vast shady hills between America and Albion's shore,
Now barr'd out by the Atlantic sea, call'd Atlantean hills,
Because from their bright summits you may pass to the Golden World,
An ancient palace, archetype of mighty Emperies,
Rears its immortal pinnacles, built in the forest of God
By Ariston, the King of Beauty, for his stolen bride.
Here on their magic seats the Thirteen Angels sat perturb'd,
For clouds from the Atlantic hover o'er the solemn roof.
Fiery the Angels rose, and as they rose deep thunder roll'd
Around their shores, indignant burning with the fires of Orc;
And Boston's Angel cried aloud as they flew thro' the dark night.

Observations

William Blake was one of the first of the Romantic poets—visionary scribes who came out of the Enlightenment with a great appreciation of the power of nature and the possibilities of humanity. Blake took things one step further than his fellow Romantics like Samuel Taylor Coleridge, William Wordsworth, Dorothy Wordsworth, Percy Bysshe Shelley, Mary Wollstonecraft Shelley, and George Gordon, Lord Byron: he was also an accomplished artist, and his poems were engraved on plates and surrounded by lush, beautiful artwork that magnificently complemented the words. (Blake's artwork is very much the spiritual ancestor of the work of Charles Vess and Brian Froud.)

"America a Prophecy" was Blake's 1793 meditation on the American Revolution, a development that Blake was very much in favor of despite his status as a British citizen. An epic poem that required eighteen engraved plates. The powerful, rousing verse, of which the excerpt above is a particularly strong example, compares the formation of the United States with well-known Biblical mythology (Moses freeing the Israelites from Egypt, Lucifer rebelling against God), with Norse mythology (references to dragons surrounding the Earth and an ash that represents the world, which seem to refer to Jörmungandr, the Midgard Serpent, and Yggdrasil, the World-Tree that connects the Nine Worlds), and with Blake's own self-created mythologies (the demiurge Urizen, and the chaotic Orc). The artwork includes images of fiery conflict, but also ones of hope amidst the greenery of nature.

Blake's epic is a classic piece of Romantic verse, a product of a turbulent time when science and democracy were on the rise, challenging the influence of religion and monarchy. "America" doesn't soft-pedal the violence inherent in that change but embraces the hope and greater future it embodies as well.

About Keith R.A. DeCandido

Keith R.A. DeCandido (DeCandido.net) is the author of more than sixty novels, more than one hundred short stories, more than fifty comic books, and more nonfiction than he's comfortable counting. His new fantasy series, Supernatural Crimes Unit, will debut in 2025 from Blackstone Publishing's Weird Tales Presents imprint, and he regularly writes about pop culture for the award-winning web site *Reactor Magazine* (formerly Tor.com).

"Annabel Lee"
by Edgar Allan Poe
Selected and with Commentary
by Alma Katsu

It was many and many a year ago,
In a kingdom by the sea,
That a maiden there lived whom you may know
By the name of Annabel Lee;
And this maiden she lived with no other thought
Than to love and be loved by me.

I was a child and *she* was a child,
In this kingdom by the sea,
But we loved with a love that was more than love—
I and my Annabel Lee—
With a love that the wingèd seraphs of Heaven
Coveted her and me.

And this was the reason that, long ago,
In this kingdom by the sea,
A wind blew out of a cloud, chilling
My beautiful Annabel Lee;
So that her highborn kinsmen came
And bore her away from me,

To shut her up in a sepulchre
In this kingdom by the sea.
The angels, not half so happy in Heaven,
Went envying her and me—
Yes!—that was the reason (as all men know,
In this kingdom by the sea)

That the wind came out of the cloud by night,
Chilling and killing my Annabel Lee.
But our love it was stronger by far than the love
Of those who were older than we—
Of many far wiser than we—
And neither the angels in Heaven above
Nor the demons down under the sea
Can ever dissever my soul from the soul
Of the beautiful Annabel Lee;

For the moon never beams, without bringing me dreams
Of the beautiful Annabel Lee;
And the stars never rise, but I feel the bright eyes
Of the beautiful Annabel Lee;
And so, all the night-tide, I lie down by the side
Of my darling—my darling—my life and my bride,
In her sepulchre there by the sea—
In her tomb by the sounding sea.

Observations

"Annabel Lee" is widely cited as the last poem Poe wrote, and it was published a few days after his death in 1849. What is mostly debated about the poem is its inspiration, as Poe had suffered the loss of many women in his life over the years, including his mother Eliza and his wife Virginia. Pinpointing his inspiration for the poem hardly seems to matter, however, as the death of young women was a recurring motif in Poe's work.

There are two ways to read this poem. One is at face value, that it is about a love forged in childhood that was so strong that the heavens were jealous and ultimately caused the death of the beloved Annabel Lee. Because the narrator cannot let his love die, he spends every night lying next to her in her sepulchre. It can be read as the ultimate love story—indeed, as the romantic ideal implanted in our minds when we first encounter the poem in high school lit.

However, this is Poe we're talking about, an over-the-top romantic with a nuclear-grade fascination with death. Could the narrator of the poem be unreliable—indeed, deranged, undone by grief? By modern standards, the poem's take on love seems immature, even a toxic over-romanticization of love. But if you understand the narrator is deranged, it aligns "Annabel Lee" with the rest of Poe's work, another nightmare from the mind of a man driven insane by loss, longing, and guilt.

About Alma Katsu

Alma Katsu is the award-winning author of eight novels, including historical horror (*The Hunger*, *The Deep*, and *The Fervor*). Her story, *The Wehrwolf*, won the Bram Stoker Award for best long fiction.

"Medusa's Tears"
by Dr. Janina Scarlet
An Essay on Personal Darkness

I just returned from my best friend's funeral. I do not think there is anything more terrifying than staring into the face of death, nothing more devastating than when it is the face of someone you love. It is at times like these that we might find ourselves reaching for our phone. A moment later, when the excruciating realization sets in that the one person who could help us process this insurmountable loss is the very person we cannot reach now, our heart breaks again.

And again.

When our grief is too massive to make sense of and too big to be allowed, we might shut down, numb out, and dissociate. In the short-term, taking a step back from grief can be helpful, even healthy, because it can give us the breathing room that we need to face it over time. But if we keep running from grief for too long, it can stay in our body and show up as nausea, muscle pain, migraines, chest tightness, panic attacks, and depression. So then, how do we stop running from this monster without it swallowing us whole?

To face our grief, we do not need to look directly into the eyes of Medusa. Instead, it is okay to use a shield to protect ourselves but to continue to face the monster anyway. And when we face it long enough, we might realize that this Medusa is not a monster after all. It is our inner friend, our own inner child crying out for love, support, and connection.

One helpful shield that we can utilize to help us cope with the enormity of grief is dark fiction. Seeing a representation of our grief in a fictional character can give us enough of a safety filter to process our own experiences in a tolerable and cathartic way. As if grieving side by side with a fictional character, we can slowly begin to open our heart to not only grief, but also to the love that is left behind when someone dies. A love that lives on forever.

And so, if you have ever dealt with your own grief and trauma by deep diving into dark fiction or rereading your favorite horror stories, please know that this is you being wise with your grief process. This is you finding a way to face your grief and to be authentic with your healing process. This kind of authenticity and the ability to face the shadows of our own past is one of the most courageous acts that we are capable of as human beings.

If you are struggling with your grief process, please know that you are not alone in feeling this way. And if you turn to dark fiction for comfort, please know that it is a brilliant way to grieve.

Thank you for being the incredible and the courageous person that you are. Thank you for being wonderful.

About Dr. Janina Scarlet

Dr. Janina Scarlet is a Licensed Clinical Psychologist, author, and a TEDx speaker. A Ukrainian-born refugee, she survived Chernobyl radiation and persecution. She immigrated to the United States at the age of twelve with her family and later, inspired by the X-Men, developed *Superhero Therapy* to help patients with anxiety, depression, and PTSD. Dr. Scarlet is the recipient of the Eleanor Roosevelt Human Rights Award by the United Nations Association for her work on *Superhero Therapy*. Her work has been featured on Yahoo, BBC, NPR; in the *Sunday Times*, *The New York Times*, *Forbes*, and in many other outlets. She regularly consults on books and television shows, including HBO's *The Young Justice*. She was also interviewed for Marvel's *MPower* series and was portrayed as a comic book character in Gail Simone's *Seven Days* graphic novel. Dr. Scarlet is the Lead Trauma Specialist at the Trauma and PTSD Healing Center.

"ANTIGONISH"
BY WILLIAM HUGHES MEARNS
SELECTED AND WITH COMMENTARY
BY JESSICA MCHUGH

Yesterday, upon the stair
I met a man who wasn't there
He wasn't there again today
I wish, I wish he'd go away...
When I came home last night at three
The man was waiting there for me
But when I looked around the hall
I couldn't see him there at all!
Go away, go away, don't you come back any more!
Go away, go away, and please don't slam the door... (slam!)
Last night I saw upon the stair
A little man who wasn't there
He wasn't there again today
Oh, how I wish he'd go away...

OBSERVATIONS

My introduction to William Hughes Mearns's "Antigonish" came in 1998 with the Todd Haynes film, *Velvet Goldmine*, a story about a pop idol's self-destruction while performing under multiple personas. Identity is a similar theme in Mearns's poem, and one I relish exploring, particularly in genres that lean into the strange and unusual. Using a simple rhyming scheme, "Antigonish" creates a complex sense of dread about a persistent presence in the narrator's home. In the context of the piece, it's unclear whether the man who wasn't there represents a literal ghost, a memory, or a past version of the narrator, but I find the ambiguity contributes to the overall unsettling nature of the poem.

About Jessica McHugh

Jessica McHugh is a two-time Bram Stoker Award-nominated poet, a multi-genre novelist, and an internationally produced playwright who spends her days surrounded by artistic inspiration at a Maryland tattoo shop. She's had thirty books published in fifteen years, including her Elgin Award-nominated blackout poetry collections, *A Complex Accident of Life* and *Strange Nests*; her sci-fi bizarro romp, *The Green Kangaroos*; and her cross-generational horror series, the Gardening Guidebooks Trilogy. Explore the growing worlds of Jessica McHugh at McHughniverse.com.

"Ah, Are You Digging on My Grave" by Thomas Hardy

Selected and with Commentary by Gregory Frost

"Ah, are you digging on my grave,
My loved one?—planting rue?"
—"No: yesterday he went to wed
One of the brightest wealth has bred.
'It cannot hurt her now,' he said,
'That I should not be true.'"

"Then who is digging on my grave?
My nearest dearest kin?"
—"Ah, no; they sit and think, 'What use!
What good will planting flowers produce?
No tendance of her mound can loose
Her spirit from Death's gin.'"

"But some one digs upon my grave?
My enemy?—prodding sly?"
—"Nay: when she heard you had passed the Gate
That shuts on all flesh soon or late,
She thought you no more worth her hate,
And cares not where you lie."

"Then, who is digging on my grave?
Say—since I have not guessed!"
—"O it is I, my mistress dear,
Your little dog, who still lives near,
And much I hope my movements here

Have not disturbed your rest?"

"Ah, yes! You dig upon my grave ...
Why flashed it not to me
That one true heart was left behind!
What feeling do we ever find
To equal among human kind
A dog's fidelity!"

"Mistress, I dug upon your grave
To bury a bone, in case
I should be hungry near this spot
When passing on my daily trot.
I am sorry, but I quite forgot
It was your resting-place."

Observations

I love the slyness of this poem of Hardy's, taking ghostly graveyard elements and making something unexpected with them, but no less strange for that.

Right off we're dealing with the dead, a spirit who wants to know who is digging on her grave. Is it her lover planting flowers, or a family member digging her up? Is it an enemy come to violate her eternal rest? And so forth. And when she learns it is her faithful dog who digs at her grave, immediately she assumes the dog's devotion to its mistress—her pet, loving her unconditionally, cannot bear that she is gone ... a riff on all the Greyfriars Bobbys in the world ... Only even here she is wrong, and the dog is simply looking to bury a bone in the boneyard.

So, while not as dark as something by Poe or Baudelaire (and lots of poems to choose from there), it still speaks to the brevity of our time and the very human tendency to assume we were important enough that someone might violate our eternal slumber, when, in fact, we are quite as forgotten as, say, whoever occupies the next plot over.

About Gregory Frost

Gregory Frost is an American writer of fantasy, horror, and science fiction. His latest work is the Rhymer trilogy from Baen Books. His fantasy novel, *Shadowbridge*, was an American Library Association Best Fantasy Novel pick. Frost has won an Asimov's Readers Award (in collaboration with Michael Swanwick) and been a finalist for Best Novel and/or Best Short

Story for the World Fantasy, Stoker, Nebula, Hugo, James Tiptree, International Horror Guild, and Theodore Sturgeon Awards. He taught the Fiction Writing Workshop at Swarthmore College for eighteen years and is a founding member of the Philadelphia Liars Club. In conjunction with Book View Café, he has e-published the short story collection *The Girlfriends of Dorian Gray & Other Stories* (originally a Golden Gryphon collection) and the Celtic fantasy novel *Táin*.

"Because I Could Not Stop for Death"
by Emily Dickinson
Selected and with Commentary by Z Brewer

Poem #479

Because I could not stop for Death—
He kindly stopped for me—
The Carriage held but just Ourselves—
And Immortality.

We slowly drove—He knew no haste
And I had put away
My labor and my leisure too,
For His Civility—

We passed the School, where Children strove
At Recess—in the Ring—
We passed the Fields of Gazing Grain—
We passed the Setting Sun—

Or rather—He passed us—
The Dews drew quivering and Chill—
For only Gossamer, my Gown—
My Tippet—only Tulle—

We paused before a House that seemed
A Swelling of the Ground—
The Roof was scarcely visible—
The Cornice—in the Ground—

Since then—'tis Centuries—and yet
Feels shorter than the Day
I first surmised the Horses' Heads
Were toward Eternity—

OBSERVATIONS

Emily Dickinson's "Because I Could Not Stop for Death" is a haunting exploration of mortality that transcends time and speaks to the universal human experience. Through her distinctive use of language and imagery, Dickinson invites readers on a journey alongside Death, personified as a courteous carriage driver. The poem opens with the speaker's reflection on their inability to halt for Death, suggesting a reluctance or perhaps fear of the inevitable. But there is one constancy, one inevitability that we all must face, whether we're comfortable with it or not: our ultimate end. No matter how we feel or what we think, one day that carriage will roll up for each of us and we *will* climb inside. It's unavoidable.

As the poem unfolds, Dickinson masterfully guides us through the stages of life and death, painting a vivid picture of the passage into eternity. The journey becomes a metaphorical voyage through time, with the speaker observing scenes of life's fleeting moments: the labor of fields, the setting sun, and the chill of dusk. Despite the solemn subject matter, there's a quiet serenity in Dickinson's portrayal of Death, as if it's not a terrifying end but rather a gentle transition into the unknown. If Ms. Dickinson offered this poem as a comfort, it's a comfort I'll take: to think of death not as a transition we should fear, but instead as a gentle journey to a new state of being.

At its core, "Because I Could Not Stop for Death" is a meditation on the cyclical nature of existence and the inevitability of our mortality. Dickinson's contemplation of eternity and the afterlife resonates deeply, prompting readers to confront their own perceptions of death and what lies beyond. Through its timeless themes and evocative imagery, this poem remains a poignant reminder of the fragility of life and the mysteries that await us all.

About Z Brewer

Z Brewer is *The New York Times* bestselling author best known for their popular young adult series the Chronicles of Vladimir Tod. They've published eight additional novels, as well as more short stories than they can recall. Their pronouns are they/them. When not making readers cry because they killed off a beloved character, Z is an anti-bullying and mental health advocate. Plus, they have awesome hair. You can learn more about Z at their website zbrewerbooks.com.

"Bothwell's Bonny Jane" by Matthew G. Lewis

Selected and with Commentary by Lisa Morton

Loud roars the north round Bothwell's hall,
And fast descends the pattering rain:
But streams of tears still faster fall
From thy blue eyes, oh! bonny Jane!

Hark! hark!—I hear, with mournful yell,
Thy wraiths[1] of angry Clyde complain;
But sorrow bursts with louder swell
From thy fair breast, oh! bonny Jane!

"Tap!—tap!"—who knocks?—the door unfolds;
The mourner lifts her melting eye,
And soon with joy and hope beholds
A reverend monk approaching nigh:

His air is mild, his step is slow,
His hands across his breast are laid,
And soft he sighs, while bending low,
—"St. Bothan[2] guard thee, gentle maid!"—

To meet the friar the damsel ran;
She kiss'd his hand, she clasp'd his knee.
'—'Now free me, free me, holy man,
'Who com'st from Blantyre Prio-rie!'—

---

1. Water-spirits
2. The patron Saint of Bothwell.

—"What mean these piteous cries, daughter?
"St. Bothan be thy speed!
"Why swim in tears thine eyes, daughter?
"From whom would'st thou be freed?"—

—'Oh! father, father! know, my sire,
'Though long I knelt, and wept, and sigh'd,
'Hath sworn, ere twice ten days expire,
'His Jane shall be Lord Malcolm's bride!'—

"Lord Malcolm is rich and great, daughter,—
"And comes of an high degree;
"He's fit to be thy mate, daughter,
"So, Benedicite!"—

'—'Oh! father, father! say not so!
'Though rich his halls, though fair his bowers,—
'There stands an hut, where Tweed doth flow,
'I prize beyond Lord Malcolm's towers:

'There dwells a youth where Tweed doth glide,
'On whom nor rank, nor fortune smiles;
'I'd rather be that peasant's bride,
'Than reign o'er all Lord Malcolm's isles.'—

—"But should you flee away, daughter,
"And wed with a village clown,
"What would your father say, daughter?
"How would he fume and frown?"—

—'Oh! he might frown and he might fume,
'And Malcolm's heart might grieve and pine,
'So Edgar's hut for me had room,
'And Edgar's lips were press'd to mine!'—

—"If at the castle gate, daughter,
"At night, thy love so true
"Should with a courser wait, daughter, ...
"What, daughter, would'st thou do?"—

'—'With noiseless step the stairs I'd press,
'Unclose the gate, and mount with glee,
'And ever, as on I sped, would bless
'The abbot of Blantyre Prio-rie!'—

—"Then, daughter, dry those eyes so bright;
"I'll haste where flows Tweed's silver stream;
"And when thou see'st, at dead of night,
"A lamp in Blantyre's chapel gleam,

"With noiseless step the staircase press,
"For know, thy lover there will be;
"Then mount his steed, haste on,—and bless
"The abbot of Blantyre Prio-rie!"—

Then forth the friar he bent his way,
While lightly danc'd the damsel's heart;
Oh! how she chid the length of day,
How sigh'd to see the sun depart!

How joy'd she when eve's shadows came,
How swiftly gain'd her tower so high!—
—'Does there in Blantyre shine a flame?—
'Ah no!—the moon deceiv'd mine eye!'—

Again the shades of evening lour;
Again she hails the approach of night.
'—'Shines there a flame in Blantyre tower?—
'Ah no!—'tis but the northern-light!'—

But when arriv'd All-hallow-E'en,[3]
What time the night and morn divide,
The signal-lamp by Jane was seen
To glimmer on the waves of Clyde.

She cares not for her father's tears,
She feels not for her father's sighs;
No voice but headstrong Love's she hears,
And down the staircase swift she hies.

Though thrice the Brownie[4] shriek'd—"Beware!"—
Though thrice was heard a dying groan,
She op'd the castle gate.—Lo! there
She found the friendly monk alone.

---

3. On this night, witches, devils, &c. are thought, by the Scots, to be abroad on their baneful errands. See Burn's Poem, under the title of "Hallowe'en."
4. The brownie is a domestic spirit, whose voice is always heard lamenting, when any accident is about to befall the family to which she has attached herself.

'—'Oh! where is Edgar, father, say?'—
—"On! on!" the friendly monk replied;
"He fear'd his berry-brown steed should neigh,
"And waits us on the banks of Clyde."—

Then on they hurried, and on they hied,
Down Bothwell's slope so steep and green,
And soon they reach'd the river's side—
Alas! no Edgar yet was seen!

Then, bonny Jane, thy spirits sunk;
Fill'd was thy heart with strange alarms!
—"Now thou art mine!" exclaim'd the monk,
And clasp'd her in his ruffian arms.

"Know, yonder bark must bear thee straight,
"Where Blantyre owns my gay controul:
"There Love and Joy to greet thee wait,
"There Pleasure crowns for thee her bowl.

"Long have I loved thee, bonny Jane,
"Long breathed to thee my secret vow!
"Come then, sweet maid!—nay, strife is vain;
"Not heaven itself can save thee now!"—

The damsel shriek'd, and would have fled,
When lo! his poniard press'd her throat!
—"One cry, and 'tis your last!"—he said,
And bore her fainting tow'rds the boat.

The moon shone bright; the winds were chain'd;
The boatman swiftly plied his oar;
But ere the river's midst was gain'd,
The tempest-fiend was heard to roar.

Rain fell in sheets; high swell'd the Clyde;
Blue flam'd the lightning's blasting brand!
—"Oh! lighten the bark!" the boatman cried,
"Or hope no more to reach the strand.

"E'en now we stand on danger's brink!
"E'en now the boat half fill'd I see!
"Oh! lighten it soon, or else we sink!
"Oh! lighten it of . . . . your gay la-die!"—

With shrieks the maid his counsel hears;
But vain are now *her* prayers and cries,
Who cared not for her father's tears,
Who felt not for her father's sighs!

Fear conquer'd love!—In wild despair
The abbot view'd the watery grave,
Then seized his victim's golden hair,
And plunged her in the foaming wave!

She screams!—she sinks!—"Row, boatman, row!
"The bark is light!" the abbot cries;
"Row, boatman, row to land!"—When lo!
Gigantic grew the boatman's size!

With burning steel his temples bound
Throbb'd quick and high with fiery pangs;
He roll'd his blood-shot eyeballs round,
And furious gnash'd his iron fangs:

His hands two gore-fed scorpions grasp'd;
His eyes fell joy and spite express'd.
—"Thy cup is full!"—he said, and clasp'd
The abbot to his burning breast.

With hideous yell down sinks the boat,
And straight the warring winds subside;
Moon-silver'd clouds through æther float,
And gently murmuring flows the Clyde.

Since then full many a winter's powers
In chains of ice the earth have bound;
And many a spring, with blushing flowers
And herbage gay, has robed the ground:

Yet legends say, at Hallow-E'en,
When Silence holds her deepest reign,
That still the ferryman-fiend is seen
To waft the monk and bonny Jane:

And still does Blantyre's wreck display
The signal-lamp at midnight hour;
And still to watch its fatal ray,
The phantom-fair haunts Bothwell Tower;

Still tunes her lute to Edgar's name,
Still chides the hours which stay her flight;
Still sings,—"In Blantyre shines the flame?
"Ah! no!—'tis but the northern-light!"—

OBSERVATIONS

Bothwell Castle is beautifully situated upon the Clyde and fronts the ruins of Blantyre Priory. The estate of Bothwell has long been, and continues to be, in the possession of the Douglas family.

Although Matthew Gregory Lewis (1775-1818) is now known mainly as the Bad Boy of Gothic Literature thanks to the publication of his scandalous classic *The Monk* (1796), he was also a fine poet whose 1801 collection *Tales of Wonder* includes one of the earliest narrative poems set on Halloween, the deliciously atmospheric and tragic "Bothwell's Bonny Jane." Apparently, Lewis was inspired to write this ballad after visiting Bothwell Castle in Scotland and hearing the legend of the doomed Jane. That legend is still around in the 21st century, with visitors to the castle sometimes claiming sightings (and even photographs!) of both Jane's spirit and the ferryman.

The poem is reproduced here with Lewis's introduction and original footnotes (note that he had to explain to his 19th-century readers what Halloween was!).

ABOUT LISA MORTON

Lisa Morton is a screenwriter, author of nonfiction books, and prose writer whose work was described by the American Library Association's *Readers' Advisory Guide to Horror* as "consistently dark, unsettling, and frightening." She is a six-time winner of the Bram Stoker Award, the author of four novels and two hundred short stories, and a world-class Halloween and paranormal expert. Her recent releases include *Calling the Spirits: A History of Seances* and *The Art of the Zombie Movie*; forthcoming in 2024 is *Placerita*, a novella co-written with John Palisano. Lisa lives in Los Angeles and online at lisamorton.com.

"A Brown Girl Dead"
by Countee Cullen
Selected and with Commentary
by Lucy Snyder

With two white roses on her breasts,
White candles at head and feet,
Dark Madonna of the grave she rests;
Lord Death has found her sweet.
Her mother pawned her wedding ring
To lay her out in white;
She'd be so proud she'd dance and sing
To see herself tonight.

Observations

"A Brown Girl Dead" is part of Countee Cullen's first published book of poetry *Color*, which was released by Harper and Brothers in 1925. Cullen was just twenty-two years old; he wrote most of the poems in the collection when he was an undergraduate at New York University. *Color* deals with major themes like race, class, religion, and injustice, and was ultimately seen as one of the major works of the Harlem Renaissance movement.

This short poem can seem deceptively simple on first reading, particularly if it's read without the context of the other poems in Cullen's collection (as it is being read here). And an out-of-context reading might make it seem as though the poem is about an innocent girl who has tragically died young and yet found a kind of wish-fulfilling redemption in death. But in the context of the themes of Cullen's work—and the pointed irony and sarcasm he often employs—this poem takes on a very different tone. The mother who has hocked her wedding ring, likely her most precious possession, to lay her dead daughter out in white (the color of

Anglo-Saxon Christian purity) is obviously suffering from internalized racism. And her going to such lengths to make her dead child seem as white as possible is deeply ironic because white society seldom pays any attention to brown kids who die young unless something particularly lurid has happened. Further, the "dance and sing" in the final couplet casts shades of the minstrel shows put on by white actors in blackface who performed caricatures of singing, dancing slaves. So, there's a further layer in that final couplet: the young woman, who was part of Cullen's generation and shared his awareness of racism, would be horrified by the pointlessly expensive white funeral her mother has laid her to rest in.

About Lucy Snyder

Lucy A. Snyder is the Shirley Jackson Award-nominated and five-time Bram Stoker Award-winning author of fifteen books and one hundred published poems. Her most recent books are the novel *Sister, Maiden, Monster* and the poetry collection *Exposed Nerves*. She lives in Columbus, Ohio, with a small jungle of houseplants, a proliferation of aquariums, and an insomnia of housemates. You can learn more about her at lucysnyder.com.

"The Waste Land: The Burial of the Dead" by T.S. Eliot

Selected and with Commentary by John Palisano

April is the cruelest month, breeding
Lilacs out of the dead land, mixing
Memory and desire, stirring
Dull roots with spring rain.
Winter kept us warm, covering
Earth in forgetful snow, feeding
A little life with dried tubers.
Summer surprised us, coming over the Starnbergersee
With a shower of rain; we stopped in the colonnade,
And went on in sunlight, into the Hofgarten
And drank coffee, and talked for an hour.
Bin gar keine Russin, stamm' aus Litauen, echt deutsch.
And when we were children, staying at the archduke's,
My cousin's, he took me out on a sled,
And I was frightened. He said, Marie,
Marie, hold on tight. And down we went.
In the mountains, there you feel free.
I read, much of the night, and go south in the winter.

What are the roots that clutch, what branches grow
Out of this stony rubbish? Son of man,
You cannot say, or guess, for you know only
A heap of broken images, where the sun beats,
And the dead tree gives no shelter, the cricket no relief,
And the dry stone no sound of water. Only
There is shadow under this red rock,
(Come in under the shadow of this red rock),
And I will show you something different from either

Your shadow at morning striding behind you
Or your shadow at evening rising to meet you;
I will show you fear in a handful of dust.
Frish weht der Wind
Der Heimat zu
Mein Irisch Kind,
Wo weilest du?
'You gave me hyacinths first a year ago;
They called me the hyacinth girl.'
—Yet when we came back, late, from the Hyacinth garden,
Your arms full, and your hair wet, I could not
Speak, and my eyes failed, I was neither
Living nor dead, and I knew nothing,
Looking into the heart of light, the silence.
Oed' und leer das Meer.

Madame Sosostris, famous clairvoyante,
Had a bad cold, nevertheless
Is known to be the wisest woman in Europe,
With a wicked pack of cards. Here, said she,
Is your card, the drowned Phoenician Sailor,
(Those are pearls that were his eyes. Look!)
Here is Belladonna, the Lady of the Rocks,
The lady of situations.
Here is the man with three staves, and here the Wheel,
And here is the one-eyed merchant, and this card,
Which is blank, is something he carries on his back,
Which I am forbidden to see. I do not find
The Hanged Man. Fear death by water.
I see crowds of people, walking round in a ring.
Thank you. If you see dear Mrs. Equitone,
Tell her I bring the horoscope myself:
One must be so careful these days.

Unreal City
Under the brown fog of a winter dawn,
A crowd flowed over London Bridge, so many,
I had not thought death had undone so many.
Sighs, short and infrequent, were exhaled,
And each man fixed his eyes before his feet.
Flowed up the hill and down King William Street,
To where Saint Mary Woolnoth kept the hours
With a dead sound on the final stroke of nine.
There I saw one I knew, and stopped him, crying 'Stetson!
'You who were with me in the ships at Mylae

'That corpse you planted last year in your garden,
'Has it begun to sprout? Will it bloom this year?
'Or has the sudden frost disturbed its bed?
'O keep the Dog far hence, that's friend to men,
'Or with his nails he'll dig it up again!
'You! hypocrite lecteur!—mon semblable,—mon frere!'

OBSERVATIONS

Like countless others, I came to read T.S. Eliot's "The Waste Land" in high school. As soon as I saw the title of the piece and the subtitle "The Burial of the Dead," I was intrigued. This was not the gentle descriptive poetry we'd been assigned up to that point. This was dark. It didn't rhyme in the same direct ways we'd come to expect.

This was the first poem I encountered with story elements and multiple characters. Such vivid images were painted so economically. The bare world of winter is just about to give way to spring, but the lack of life is a reminder of nature's cycles, and our own. "April is the cruelest month." One of the most unforgettable opening lines. Another, "I will show you fear in a handful of dust," a chilling reminder of our own mortality. This was not kids' stuff. This was deep. And the last stanza of the first section, as our narrator meets with living embodiments of the tarot deck, with a scene that will return again, like a theme in a symphony—The Unreal City. Where seeds are compared to corpses that, when planted, will sprout and grow. Unless they are found and dug up by wild dogs.

There's so much to unpack in every line. "The Waste Land" is dense, with clues to larger events and stories. It drops verses in Latin, French, and German, insisting the reader be fluent or know the references, not unlike unravelling a mystery cloaked in codes and clues, and in this case, a peek into what death has brought and where life may begin again once more. Today, in contemporary works, you can feel its influence. It gives no easy answers, and the ones you'll find are the ones it evokes from you.

ABOUT JOHN PALISANO

John Palisano's writing has appeared in venues such as *Cemetery Dance*, *Fangoria*, *Weird Tales*, *Space & Time*, and McFarland Press. He's been quoted in *Vanity Fair*, the *Los Angeles Times*, and *The Writer*. He's been awarded the Bram Stoker Award, the Yog Soggoth Award, and more, and served as president of the Horror Writers Association.

"CANIS MAJOR" BY ROBERT FROST
SELECTED AND WITH COMMENTARY
BY ALESSANDRO MANZETTI

The great Overdog
That heavenly beast
With a star in one eye
Gives a leap in the east.
He dances upright
All the way to the west
And never once drops
On his forefeet to rest.
I'm a poor underdog,
But to-night I will bark
With the great Overdog
That romps through the dark.

OBSERVATIONS

In this poem, Robert Frost lifts our gaze to the night sky and beyond, until our minds, illuminated by Sirius, touch the constellation that titles these verses. Here we take note (not for the first time) of the dark cosmos, which seems ever-large and always too black to be real.

The figure of the Overdog represents both the universe and the unknown. The observer represents our desire to connect to the arcane forces from whence we feel we originate: all those stars and planets up there, so immobile and eternally silent; yet the Overdog at any moment seems to move in front of the man, leaping like a wild animal. The verses carry a sonic sense of different leaps, as the beast bounds toward something fascinating.

Barking at the universe, as a werewolf would to the face of the moon, represents a human protest, a shout: we want an answer from that vast entity which contains us, which seems so foreign to us, yet also seems to be a part of us. We sense these infinitesimal elements,/ growling at them like frightened dogs from the first day we set foot on this planet.

About Alessandro Manzetti

Alessandro Manzetti is a three-time Bram Stoker Award-winning writer, editor, scriptwriter, and essayist of horror fiction and dark poetry. His work has been published extensively, with more than forty books appearing in Italian and in English, including novels, short and long fiction, poetry, essays, graphic novels, and collections. Website: battiago.com.

"Childe Roland to the Dark Tower Came" by Robert Browning
Selected and with Commentary by John Langan

(Excerpted sections 1-8, 27-34)

I.
My first thought was, he lied in every word,
That hoary cripple, with malicious eye
Askance to watch the working of his lie
On mine, and mouth scarce able to afford
Suppression of the glee, that pursed and scored
Its edge, at one more victim gained thereby.

II.
What else should he be set for, with his staff?
What, save to waylay with his lies, ensnare
All travellers who might find him posted there,
And ask the road? I guessed what skull-like laugh
Would break, what crutch 'gin write my epitaph
For pastime in the dusty thoroughfare,

III.
If at his counsel I should turn aside
Into that ominous tract which, all agree,
Hides the Dark Tower. Yet acquiescingly
I did turn as he pointed: neither pride
Nor hope rekindling at the end descried,
So much as gladness that some end might be.

IV.
For, what with my whole world-wide wandering,

What with my search drawn out thro' years, my hope
Dwindled into a ghost not fit to cope
With that obstreperous joy success would bring,
I hardly tried now to rebuke the spring
My heart made, finding failure in its scope.

V.
As when a sick man very near to death
Seems dead indeed, and feels begin and end
The tears and takes the farewell of each friend,
And hears one bid the other go, draw breath
Freelier outside, ("since all is o'er," he saith,
"And the blow fallen no grieving can amend,")

VI.
While some discuss if near the other graves
Be room enough for this, and when a day
Suits best for carrying the corpse away,
With care about the banners, scarves and staves:
And still the man hears all, and only craves
He may not shame such tender love and stay.

VII.
Thus, I had so long suffered in this quest,
Heard failure prophesied so oft, been writ
So many times among "The Band"—to wit,
The knights who to the Dark Tower's search addressed
Their steps—that just to fail as they, seemed best,
And all the doubt was now—should I be fit?

VIII.
So, quiet as despair, I turned from him,
That hateful cripple, out of his highway
Into the path he pointed. All the day
Had been a dreary one at best, and dim
Was settling to its close, yet shot one grim
Red leer to see the plain catch its estray.

XXVII.
And just as far as ever from the end!
Nought in the distance but the evening, nought
To point my footstep further! At the thought,
A great black bird, Apollyon's bosom-friend,
Sailed past, nor beat his wide wing dragon-penned
That brushed my cap—perchance the guide I sought.

XXVIII.
For, looking up, aware I somehow grew,
'Spite of the dusk, the plain had given place
All round to mountains—with such name to grace
Mere ugly heights and heaps now stolen in view.
How thus they had surprised me,—solve it, you!
How to get from them was no clearer case.

XXIX.
Yet half I seemed to recognize some trick
Of mischief happened to me, God knows when—
In a bad dream perhaps. Here ended, then,
Progress this way. When, in the very nick
Of giving up, one time more, came a click
As when a trap shuts—you're inside the den!

XXX.
Burningly it came on me all at once,
This was the place! those two hills on the right,
Crouched like two bulls locked horn in horn in fight;
While to the left, a tall scalped mountain ... Dunce,
Dotard, a-dozing at the very nonce,
After a life spent training for the sight!

XXXI.
What in the midst lay but the Tower itself?
The round squat turret, blind as the fool's heart,
Built of brown stone, without a counterpart
In the whole world. The tempest's mocking elf
Points to the shipman thus the unseen shelf
He strikes on, only when the timbers start.

XXXII.
Not see? because of night perhaps?—why, day
Came back again for that! before it left,
The dying sunset kindled through a cleft:
The hills, like giants at a hunting, lay,
Chin upon hand, to see the game at bay,—
"Now stab and end the creature—to the heft!"

XXXIII.
Not hear? when noise was everywhere! it tolled
Increasing like a bell. Names in my ears
Of all the lost adventurers my peers,—
How such a one was strong, and such was bold,

And such was fortunate, yet, each of old
Lost, lost! one moment knelled the woe of years.

XXXIV.
There they stood, ranged along the hill-sides, met
To view the last of me, a living frame
For one more picture! in a sheet of flame
I saw them and I knew them all. And yet
Dauntless the slug-horn to my lips I set,
And blew. "Childe Roland to the Dark Tower came."

Observations

I first became aware of Robert Browning's great, weird poem "Childe Roland to the Dark Tower Came" through reading *The Gunslinger*, the first volume of Stephen King's Dark Tower sequence of novels and stories and *Stephen King: The Art of Darkness*, in Douglas Winter's study while I was in high school. Winter mentioned Browning's dramatic monologue as an important influence on King's cryptic novel, at that point still published only in a limited edition. It wasn't until I was an undergraduate, however, that I actually read "Childe Roland," which I found in the pages of my English Literature 2 textbook.

Despite the decades that have passed since I bent over my copy of the *Norton Anthology of English Literature* (Vol. 2), I can remember the sensation of reading the poem, which I picture as attempting to make my way through a dense, thorny thicket (an image that seems to fit the poem's gnarled imagery). There was, I could see, a story reaching its conclusion, the end of a long quest whose searchers had come to a variety of bad ends. The landscape of the poem was ominous, a sense of imminent threat, of doom, hanging over it. The speaker's perspective was bitter, ironic, expressed in knotted language that caught at me, sent me back over lines I had just read. The ending arrived in a rush, a visionary moment igniting the poem, stirring its speaker to an act simultaneously dramatic and cryptic. For all intents and purposes, the poem ended on a cliffhanger, the last line circling back to its title, returning me to its beginning.

Since that first encounter, I've spent a lot of time with the poem Robert Browning wrote on the third day of 1852, a product of his resolution to write a poem a day. I've taught it multiple times. I've thought and spoken about its influence on King's Dark Tower project. I've written the bulk of a critical study of its influence on three of H.P. Lovecraft's stories (which incorporates a study of its relation to Shakespeare's *King Lear*). I've written my own fictive response to it ("Shadow and Thirst"). With each pass, I am better able to navigate the tangles and snares of its language, its speaker's twisting perspective; indeed, I find myself admiring the accomplishment of its style. My long journey with the poem reminds me of those professors I looked up to when I was an undergraduate, who had spent their careers engaged with the work of a single writer, reading a single text over and over again. At the time, I had difficulty understanding how they could do that, how a single work of literature could occupy them so completely for such a length of time. Now I look up, and to my surprise find I have done something similar with "Childe Roland."

Even so, I am far from an expert on the poem. But aspects of it now seem clearer to me. The title, for example, whose quotation marks place it at something of a remove from the poem that follows, a remove which is confirmed by the parenthetical reference to Edgar's song in Shakespeare's *King Lear*. Half a children's nursery rhyme, Edgar's song describes a knight arriving at the dark tower, his speech (apparently) that of the giant able to smell the blood of an Englishman in the "Jack and the Beanstalk" fairytale. Within the context of Lear, the song raises a host of questions. The use of its first line here suggests an earlier expression or version of the journey Browning's poem will describe; a kind of reference point though not an exact duplicate.

Instead, the later poem begins in suspicion, as its speaker confronts a sinister old man, crippled in some way, who, in response to a request for directions the speaker has put to him utters words the speaker immediately takes for a lie. It's an ominous enough encounter whose sense begins to fray almost immediately, as the speaker, apparently on the old man's advice, turns from the road he has been traveling into the expanse of land which popular opinion agrees hides the Dark Tower—the object of the speaker's long quest. But if this is the case, then what reason is there for the speaker to suspect the old man of lying? It's the first instance of the speaker's tortured perspective, an adjective I use both in its psychological sense of tormented and its physical sense of winding. Before very long, we'll learn that while the speaker may know the general location of the Dark Tower, he has, up until this point, not found it, possibly because he has not made the attempt. This answer, though, raises another question: why has he not tried?

Even as we're contemplating a response to this, we're already well into the poem's landscape—filtered through the speaker's consciousness. Indeed, as we advance in one, so do we move deeper into the other. The speaker indulges in an elaborate, Homeric simile about failure; he revisits the dismal fates of the other members of his band of knights, fellow searchers for the Dark Tower. (Why they're looking for the structure is never made clear.) In between, he describes his voyage across the plain, whose sparse vegetation is diseased. He sees a lone horse so skeletal it appears on the far side of damnation. He fords a stream beneath whose surface his probing spear impales something that screams like a baby. He crosses earth whose trampling he takes as a sign of a recent battle. He sees a machine he assumes is an instrument of torture. The speaker's experiences in this section of the poem are marked by a sense of belatedness, of having just missed major events, of passing through a landscape of aftermath. At the same time, because the poem adheres so closely to his perspective, another possibility starts to come into focus: namely, that everything the speaker describes to us is the product of his imagination, the projection of an overheated internal fantasy onto an otherwise mundane scene.

Before we can commit too much to such an interpretation, however, the poem's ending arrives, bringing with it the Dark Tower. Startled out of his reflections by the passage of a monstrous bird overhead, the speaker realizes his surroundings have changed. From the desiccated plain, he has emerged into mountains—how, he's not quite sure—the silhouettes of which reveal that he has at last reached the site of the Dark Tower. In a poem whose many details invite discussion, the Dark Tower, the "round squat turret, blind as the fool's heart, / Built of brown stone, without a counterpart / In the whole world" suggests possibilities that would fill pages. (Trust me: I've written them.) With its appearance comes the entirety of the speaker's former companions, positioned along the mountains, wreathed in flame. It is as if his triumph has summoned them (possibly from hell) to witness it. Despite their presence—the reminder of their collective failure—the speaker raises his battle horn to his lips and sounds it. It's a defiant gesture, if a cryptic one: as the Dark Tower is blind, which is to say, without (evident) opening, it's unclear what effect blowing the horn is supposed to have vis-à-vis the structure. Who (or what) is the sound announcing the speaker to? Who (or what) is the sound summoning? And from where?

The only answer the poem gives us, however, is to return to its title. Does this mean we are supposed to return to the beginning of the poem and repeat our reading of it? (Something of this interpretation plays out in King's Dark Tower books.) Or does it direct us to Edgar's song in *King Lear*, instructing us to make our way back to the earlier version of the narrative we've just finished? In raising such questions, I don't mean to overcomplicate the poem. Perhaps the goal of the quest for the Dark Tower has always been to find it and to blow your horn there. (This is just about the way the late literary critic, Harold Bloom, understood the poem.) Somehow, though, this explanation doesn't feel adequate, doesn't feel like it's enough to fit the other details the poem has provided us. But what is? Suppose ... suppose the only way for the speaker to describe the experience that follows his sounding the slug-horn is the poem itself. What then?

About John Langan

John Langan is the author of two novels and five collections of stories. For his work, he has received the Bram Stoker and the This Is Horror Awards. One of the founders of the Shirley Jackson Award, he serves on its Board of Advisors. He lives in New York's Mid-Hudson Valley with his wife, younger son, and a pair of miniature tigers who are developing a taste for human flesh.

"Darkness" by George Gordon (Lord) Byron

Selected and with Commentary by Del Howison

I had a dream, which was not all a dream.
The bright sun was extinguish'd, and the stars
Did wander darkling in the eternal space,
Rayless, and pathless, and the icy earth
Swung blind and blackening in the moonless air;
Morn came and went—and came, and brought no day,
And men forgot their passions in the dread
Of this their desolation; and all hearts
Were chill'd into a selfish prayer for light:
And they did live by watchfires—and the thrones,
The palaces of crowned kings—the huts,
The habitations of all things which dwell,
Were burnt for beacons; cities were consum'd,
And men were gather'd round their blazing homes
To look once more into each other's face;
Happy were those who dwelt within the eye
Of the volcanos, and their mountain-torch:
A fearful hope was all the world contain'd;
Forests were set on fire—but hour by hour
They fell and faded—and the crackling trunks
Extinguish'd with a crash—and all was black.
The brows of men by the despairing light
Wore an unearthly aspect, as by fits
The flashes fell upon them; some lay down
And hid their eyes and wept; and some did rest
Their chins upon their clenched hands, and smil'd;
And others hurried to and fro, and fed
Their funeral piles with fuel, and look'd up

With mad disquietude on the dull sky,
The pall of a past world; and then again
With curses cast them down upon the dust,
And gnash'd their teeth and howl'd: the wild birds shriek'd
And, terrified, did flutter on the ground,
And flap their useless wings; the wildest brutes
Came tame and tremulous; and vipers crawl'd
And twin'd themselves among the multitude,
Hissing, but stingless—they were slain for food.
And War, which for a moment was no more,
Did glut himself again: a meal was bought
With blood, and each sate sullenly apart
Gorging himself in gloom: no love was left;
All earth was but one thought—and that was death
Immediate and inglorious; and the pang
Of famine fed upon all entrails—men
Died, and their bones were tombless as their flesh;
The meagre by the meagre were devour'd,
Even dogs assail'd their masters, all save one,
And he was faithful to a corse, and kept
The birds and beasts and famish'd men at bay,
Till hunger clung them, or the dropping dead
Lur'd their lank jaws; himself sought out no food,
But with a piteous and perpetual moan,
And a quick desolate cry, licking the hand
Which answer'd not with a caress—he died.
The crowd was famish'd by degrees; but two
Of an enormous city did survive,
And they were enemies: they met beside
The dying embers of an altar-place
Where had been heap'd a mass of holy things
For an unholy usage; they rak'd up,
And shivering scrap'd with their cold skeleton hands
The feeble ashes, and their feeble breath
Blew for a little life, and made a flame
Which was a mockery; then they lifted up
Their eyes as it grew lighter, and beheld
Each other's aspects—saw, and shriek'd, and died—
Even of their mutual hideousness they died,
Unknowing who he was upon whose brow
Famine had written Fiend. The world was void,
The populous and the powerful was a lump,
Seasonless, herbless, treeless, manless, lifeless—
A lump of death—a chaos of hard clay.
The rivers, lakes and ocean all stood still,

And nothing stirr'd within their silent depths;
Ships sailorless lay rotting on the sea,
And their masts fell down piecemeal: as they dropp'd
They slept on the abyss without a surge—
The waves were dead; the tides were in their grave,
The moon, their mistress, had expir'd before;
The winds were wither'd in the stagnant air,
And the clouds perish'd; Darkness had no need
Of aid from them—She was the Universe.

OBSERVATIONS

When I was a young child, young enough to still have parental-imposed naps, I pondered deep, dark thoughts. I remember this quite vividly. It is even odder to me now, at this later point in my life, that I would have been doing this at such a young age. But it's true. The most frequent thought that troubled my young mind was time—specifically eternity. I would lay on my mattress, eyes wide open, staring at the ceiling while contemplating death. Where would I go (meaning my inner being) when I died? I tried to equate it with where I was prior to being born. At both ends of the timeline I only arrived at darkness, nothingness. There was no context. The was no mother's hug to cling to, no father's hand to hold onto, nor even a blanket to cover me for the illusion of security.

This frightened me beyond belief. I fed my own fear of the unknown. My anxiety rose to the point of erupting, and I worried about drifting off into the semiconsciousness of sleep. I believed, if I fell asleep, I would float aimlessly in the darkness until, somehow, miraculously, I would come back to the world I knew, maybe. Where was my consciousness prior to my birth? Where would it slip to when I died? What huge void was this darkness surrounding the timeline of my life?

One day, I read the poem "Darkness" by Lord Byron. I'm sure that by then I was a teenager. In reading it I realized I was no longer alone. My fear was his fear. He calmed me with his dream. In his vision Lord Byron made my terror the panic of the entire world. We are the nucleus of nothingness no matter how large or how small we are. "She (Darkness) was the Universe."

About Del Howison

Del Howison is an author, journalist, actor (see IMDB), and the Bram Stoker Award-winning editor of the anthology *Dark Delicacies: Original Tales of Terror and the Macabre by the World's Greatest Horror Writers*. He has written articles for Fear.net, CemeteryDance.com, and *Writers Digest*, among others. His Western short story "The Lost Herd" was turned into the premiere (and highest-rated) episode, "The Sacrifice," for the series *Fear Itself*. His dark Western novel *The Survival of Margaret Thomas* was shortlisted for the Peacemaker Award given out by the Western Fictioneers. He has been shortlisted for over half a dozen awards including the Shirley Jackson Award and the Black Quill. He is the cofounder and owner (with his wife, Sue) of Dark Delicacies, a book and gift store known as "The Home of Horror," located in Burbank, California. The store won the "Il Posto Nero" Award from Italy and has been inducted into the Rondo Hatton Hall of Fame.

"Death Be Not Proud"
by John Donne
Selected and with Commentary
by Charisma Carpenter

Death, be not proud, though some have called thee
Mighty and dreadful, for thou art not so;
For those whom thou think'st thou dost overthrow
Die not, poor Death, nor yet canst thou kill me.
From rest and sleep, which but thy pictures be,
Much pleasure; then from thee much more must flow,
And soonest our best men with thee do go,
Rest of their bones, and soul's delivery.
Thou art slave to fate, chance, kings, and desperate men,
And dost with poison, war, and sickness dwell,
And poppy or charms can make us sleep as well
And better than thy stroke; why swell'st thou then?
One short sleep past, we wake eternally
And death shall be no more; Death, thou shalt die.

Observations

Immediately this poem pisses me off.
    Death *is* dreadful.
    It *is* powerful because it *does* rob us of all earthly attachments. It robs us of all things we have ever known. How is that not something to dread or fear? If one has ever loved and lost, experiencing that loss of disconnection from our attached feels intolerable.
    But what's beautiful about it is the conversation or internal consideration that we should pity death as it can never truly "get us" if we live on in spirit. In the hearts of those who outlive us. But once those people

die off, there is nothing left of us, and did we ever exist at all one hundred years later if no one knows of us? There is the afterlife, if you believe in such things, but what this poem reminds me today, is to live. Live loud, transparently, and authentically.

Make use of your time and give of yourself fully so that when you are remembered, you are remembered well and were considered of service useful to others. Death has no advantage to a legend.

About Charisma Carpenter

Charisma Carpenter is an American actress most recognizable for her work in several TV cult classics such as: *Buffy the Vampire Slayer*, the spin-off to *BTVS*, *Angel*, *Veronica Mars*, and *Charmed*. Charisma also appeared on *Supernatural*, *Lucifer*, *Sons of Anarchy*, and Ryan Murphy's *Scream Queens* and *9-1-1*. Carpenter has also segued into movies, with a supporting role as Lacey in *The Expendables* and its sequel, *The Expendables 2*, as well as roles in over twelve made-for-television movies for Lifetime, Syfy, and more. Carpenter subsequently served as host and producer of *Investigation Discovery's Surviving Evil*, a series featuring survivors who fought back against their attacker. Offscreen, Carpenter is the proud founder of MyCon, a platform intended to lift the spirits of socially isolated fans throughout the pandemic by connecting them with their favorite actors. Additionally, she works closely with the Thirst Project, an international water charity bringing safe, clean drinking water to the most vulnerable people around the world, as well as the Ronan Thompson Foundation, which is dedicated to researching pediatric cancer. In addition to her first love, that of a devoted mother, Carpenter spends much of her time working as a philanthropist, political activist, and social justice advocate. So passionate about these causes, she recently completed a course on administrative justice.

"Dulce et Decorum Est"
by Wilfred Owen
Selected and with Commentary
by Duane Swierczynski

*(Latin phrase is from the Roman poet Horace:
"It is sweet and fitting to die for one's country.")*

Bent double, like old beggars under sacks,
Knock-kneed, coughing like hags, we cursed through sludge,
Till on the haunting flares we turned our backs,
And towards our distant rest began to trudge.
Men marched asleep. Many had lost their boots,
But limped on, blood-shod. All went lame; all blind;
Drunk with fatigue; deaf even to the hoots
Of gas-shells dropping softly behind.
Gas! GAS! Quick, boys!—An ecstasy of fumbling
Fitting the clumsy helmets just in time,
But someone still was yelling out and stumbling
And flound'ring like a man in fire or lime.—
Dim through the misty panes and thick green light,
As under a green sea, I saw him drowning.
In all my dreams before my helpless sight,
He plunges at me, guttering, choking, drowning.
If in some smothering dreams, you too could pace
Behind the wagon that we flung him in,
And watch the white eyes writhing in his face,
His hanging face, like a devil's sick of sin;
If you could hear, at every jolt, the blood
Come gargling from the froth-corrupted lungs,
Obscene as cancer, bitter as the cud
Of vile, incurable sores on innocent tongues,—

My friend, you would not tell with such high zest
To children ardent for some desperate glory,
The old Lie: *Dulce et decorum est
Pro patria mori.*

Observations

"An ecstasy of fumbling"—a surreal action movie moment between the foreboding darkness and full-on horror of Wilfred Owen's unforgettable WWI poem. Those four words, when I encountered them back in college, taught me it was possible to compress entire worlds into very few words. The word "ecstasy" is key. At first, it feels like a strange word to describe the harrowing seconds right before poison gas might (or might not) fill your lungs. But that's the ecstasy part. Despite everything, you're giddy you may actually *survive*.

As is the case here, where our narrator's temporary relief turns to numb horror as a fellow soldier succumbs to bis(2-chloroethyl) sulfide. He is right there with him, yet at a remove—"dim through the misty panes and thick green light, as under a green sea."

But Wilfred Owen was there, and I consider him a journalist as much as a poet. "Dulce et Decorum Est" is reportage from a real incident on January 12, 1917. Only twenty-four at the time, Owen and his fellow soldiers (mere "boys") are presented as old men: bent over, blind, drunk, and deaf. By the poem's end, he has transformed into a ghostly herald, warning us not to believe the tired "old lie" about the glory of dying for your country. And indeed, Owen would perish in battle just a week before Armistice. His warning haunts us more than a century later. *This,* Owen tells us, *is what it's really like.*

About Duane Swierczynski

Duane Swierczynski is The New York Times bestselling and two-time Edgar-nominated author of fifteen novels including California Bear, Fun & Games, and The Wheelman, as well as the graphic novels Breakneck and John Carpenter's Tales of Science Fiction: Redhead. Along with James Patterson, Duane co-created the Audible Original The Guilty, starring John Lithgow and Bryce Dallas Howard, and co-wrote the private eye thriller Lion & Lamb. His first short story collection,

Lush & Other Tales of Boozy Mayhem, was recently published by Cimarron Street Books. A native Philadelphian, Duane now lives in Southern California with his family. Visit him at gleefulmayhem.com.

"Eldorado"
by Edgar Allan Poe
Selected and with Commentary by David Fitzgerald

Gaily bedight,
A gallant knight,
In sunshine and in shadow,
Had journeyed long,
Singing a song,
In search of Eldorado.
But he grew old—
This knight so bold—
And o'er his heart a shadow
Fell, as he found
No spot of ground
That looked like Eldorado.
And, as his strength
Failed him at length,
He met a pilgrim shadow—
'Shadow,' said he,
'Where can it be—
This land of Eldorado?'
'Over the Mountains
Of the Moon,
Down the Valley of the Shadow,
Ride, boldly ride,'
The shade replied,—
'If you seek for Eldorado!'

Observations

Several contributors beat me to the punch with other poems I love ("The Second Coming," "Dulce et Decorum Est," "Ozymandias") and I was also sorely tempted to pick one in Irish with the English translation ("Turas go Tír na nÓg," or "Maraiodh Brian Boru") but in the end, to best keep with the topic, I picked this one by Edgar Allan Poe.

It's a haunting little story of a knight grown old and a ghost; so simple and short, and yet can be read in so many different ways: Is the "knight" a rapacious conquistador being mocked by his conscience on his deathbed? Is he a Don Quixote-like figure, ever hopeful even to the end? Whatever its meaning, I've always thrilled to that last line spoken by the knight's spectral companion: "Over the Mountains Of the Moon, Down the Valley of the Shadow; Ride, boldly ride—If you seek for Eldorado!"

About David Fitzgerald

David Fitzgerald is a historical researcher, an international public speaker, and an award-winning author of both genre fiction and historical nonfiction, such as the Complete Heretic's Guide to Western Religion series and *Nailed*. He is also a founding member of San Francisco Writer's Coffeehouse, along with his wife, actress/writer Dana Fredsti. Their most recent fiction is the science fiction adventure trilogy *Time Shards*. The two also collaborated on "Maid of Steel," a dark fantasy story appearing in the Sword & Sorcery issue of *Weird Tales Magazine*, and are currently writing a grimdark novel for Weird Tales Presents/Blackstone Publishing. They live in the Victorian seaport town of Eureka, CA, (in Bigfoot country!) with a horde of felines and their dog Pogeen.

"Exile" by Winifred Welles
Selected and with Commentary by Marguerite Reed

I have made grief a gorgeous, queenly thing,
And worn my melancholy with an air.
My tears were big as stars to deck my hair,
My silence stunning as a sapphire ring.
Oh, more than any light the dark could fling
A glamour over me to make me rare,
Better than any color I could wear
The pearly grandeur that the shadows bring.
What is there left to joy for such as I?
What throne can dawn upraise for me who found
The dusk so royal and so rich a one?
Laughter will whirl and whistle on the sky—
Far from this riot I shall stand uncrowned,
Disrobed, bereft, an outcast in the sun.

Observations

I don't think Winifred Welles ever flipped someone the bird in her life. Born circa 1893 and deceased at around forty-five to forty-six years old, Welles was a New Englander, alive during the grind of World War I and the Great Depression. No biographical information tells us whether her life was happy or not—the one photograph I found of her depicts a plain woman with a determined mouth. If genealogy websites are to be believed, the paternal side of her family had been in Connecticut since the 17th century. That determined mouth was well-earned.

Yet this Miltonian sonnet, more art nouveau than art deco (for all that it was published in 1920, after Beardsley and Mucha had passed from fashion), is a big middle finger. A regal middle finger, to be sure, but no amount of filigree or gilt can conceal the poet's pain and rage. Welles's usual work included winsome canine fantasies, studies of orchard angels visiting children: verses benign enough to be published as juvenilia; other collections wistful and melancholy yet inscribed with a pen adamantine enough to save her writing from mawkishness. She wrote about fear, loneliness, and grief, but allowed the reader genteel glimpses only, as if through a frosted window, a lace curtain.

In "Exile," Welles rips aside that curtain to reveal a hurt great enough to flaunt with "glamour" and "grandeur," a hurt she could parade like jewelry. In the first eight lines—the standard sonnet octave—she employs both abstract and concrete imagery to conjure up a veritable dark fairy. Despite her pain and anger, in the volta—or turn—of the ninth line, she abjures such Gothic excess. The sonnet reaches its resolution in the acceptance of a desert banishment. One cannot help but think of Tolkien's Galadriel who imagines herself wielding ultimate power as a beautiful and terrible queen throwing all her subjects into despair—and then makes the choice "to diminish, and go into the West."

I wonder though, whether the poem's subject chose her exile, or whether that dark fairy reigning in her crepuscular palace flipped off her subjects one too many times.

About Marguerite Reed

Marguerite Reed comes from a long line of farmers and artists. She might describe herself as a medievalist but writes mostly science fiction. Her short stories have appeared in Strange Horizons and *Weird Tales*, and her SF novel *Archangel* was awarded the 2016 Philip K Dick Special Citation of Excellence.

"Full Fathom Five"
by William Shakespeare
Selected and with Commentary by Greg Cox

(Excerpted from The Tempest)

Full fathom five your father lies;
Of his bones are coral made;
Those are pearls that were his eyes:
Nothing of him that doth fade,
But doth suffer a sea-change
Into something rich and strange.

Observations

Overall, *The Tempest* is more fantasy than horror, but when it comes to the verses above, is there a better metaphor for the way that horror writers can take something grim and macabre and, through craft and artistry and imagination, transform it into something darkly beautiful? Looked at the right way, there is a sinister beauty to be found in even something as starkly grotesque as the bones of a drowned sailor, as anyone who has ever swooned over a particularly gorgeous old cemetery, looming castle, crumbling ruin, or dark, skeletal forest can attest. At its most poetic, horror fiction can find that beauty and open our eyes to its strange, seductive allure—even as it goes for our throats.

About Greg Cox

Greg Cox is a *New York Times* bestselling author and veteran book editor. On the horror front, he wrote the novelizations of the first three *Underworld* movies, coedited two anthologies of science fiction, vampire, and werewolf stories, and has edited such authors as Richard Matheson, Chelsea Quinn Yarbro, Jonathan Maberry, Seanan McGuire, S.P. Somtow, R.S. Belcher, and others. He has also written numerous media tie-in novels for such popular properties as *Batman*, *CSI: Crime Scene Investigations*, *Ghost Rider*, *Godzilla*, *Planet of the Apes*, and *Star Trek*. His first original horror novel, *Hungry as the Grave*, was recently acquired by Blackstone Publishing.

"The Cremation of Sam McGee" by Robert W. Service

Selected and with Commentary by R.L. Stine

There are strange things done in the midnight sun
By the men who moil for gold;
The Arctic trails have their secret tales
That would make your blood run cold;
The Northern Lights have seen queer sights,
But the queerest they ever did see
Was that night on the marge of Lake Lebarge
I cremated Sam McGee.

Now Sam McGee was from Tennessee, where the cotton blooms and blows.
Why he left his home in the South to roam 'round the Pole, God only knows.
He was always cold, but the land of gold seemed to hold him like a spell;
Though he'd often say in his homely way that he'd sooner live in hell.
On a Christmas Day we were mushing our way over the Dawson trail.
Talk of your cold! through the parka's fold it stabbed like a driven nail.
If our eyes we'd close, then the lashes froze till sometimes we couldn't see;
It wasn't much fun, but the only one to whimper was Sam McGee.
And that very night, as we lay packed tight in our robes beneath the snow,

And the dogs were fed, and the stars o'erhead were dancing
heel and toe,
He turned to me, and "Cap," says he, "I'll cash in this trip, I
guess;
And if I do, I'm asking that you won't refuse my last
request."
Well, he seemed so low that I couldn't say no; then he says
with a sort of moan:
"It's the cursèd cold, and it's got right hold till I'm chilled
clean through to the bone.
Yet 'tain't being dead—it's my awful dread of the icy grave
that pains;
So I want you to swear that, foul or fair, you'll cremate my
last remains."
A pal's last need is a thing to heed, so I swore I would not
fail;
And we started on at the streak of dawn; but God! he
looked ghastly pale.
He crouched on the sleigh, and he raved all day of his home
in Tennessee;
And before nightfall a corpse was all that was left of Sam
McGee.
There wasn't a breath in that land of death, and I hurried,
horror-driven,
With a corpse half hid that I couldn't get rid, because of a
promise given;
It was lashed to the sleigh, and it seemed to say: "You may
tax your brawn and brains,
But you promised true, and it's up to you to cremate those
last remains."
Now a promise made is a debt unpaid, and the trail has its
own stern code.
In the days to come, though my lips were dumb, in my heart
how I cursed that load!
In the long, long night, by the lone firelight, while the
huskies, round in a ring,
Howled out their woes to the homeless snows—O God!
how I loathed the thing!
And every day that quiet clay seemed to heavy and heavier
grow;
And on I went, though the dogs were spent and the grub
was getting low.
The trail was bad, and I felt half mad, but I swore I would
not give in;

And I'd often sing to the hateful thing, and it hearkened with a grin.
Till I came to the marge of Lake Lebarge, and a derelict there lay;
It was jammed in the ice, but I saw in a trice it was called the Alice May.
And I looked at it, and I thought a bit, and I looked at my frozen chum;
Then "Here," said I, with a sudden cry, "is my cre-ma-tor-eum!"
Some planks I tore from the cabin floor and I lit the boiler fire;
Some coal I found that was lying around, and I heaped the fuel higher;
The flames just soared, and the furnace roared—such a blaze you seldom see,
And I burrowed a hole in the glowing coal, and I stuffed in Sam McGee.
Then I made a hike, for I didn't like to hear him sizzle so;
And the heavens scowled, and the huskies howled, and the wind began to blow.
It was icy cold, but the hot sweat rolled down my cheeks, and I don't know why;
And the greasy smoke in an inky cloak went streaking down the sky.
I do not know how long in the snow I wrestled with grisly fear;
But the stars came out and they danced about ere again I ventured near;
I was sick with dread, but I bravely said, "I'll just take a peep inside.
I guess he's cooked, and it's time I looked." ... Then the door I opened wide.
And there sat Sam, looking cool and calm, in the heart of the furnace roar;
And he wore a smile you could see a mile, and he said, "Please close that door.
It's fine in here, but I greatly fear you'll let in the cold and storm—
Since I left Plumtree, down in Tennessee, it's the first time I've been warm."

There are strange things done in the midnight sun
By the men who moil for gold;
The Arctic trails have their secret tales

That would make your blood run cold;
The Northern Lights have seen queer sights,
But the queerest they ever did see
Was that night on the marge of Lake Lebarge
I cremated Sam McGee.

OBSERVATIONS

I discovered Robert W. Service's poems when I was nine or ten, and they taught me a lot about what poetry could be. They weren't like any poems I had read before. They were about hard, dangerous men in a cold, unfriendly world. The poems were tough. They made you shiver. They made my blood run cold.

If you think poems can't give you a chill, read this one. It's my all-time favorite by Service.

ABOUT R.L. STINE

R.L. Stine is one of the bestselling children's authors in history. *Goosebumps*, which recently celebrated its thirtieth anniversary, has more than 400 million books in print in thirty-two languages. An all-new, *New York Times* bestselling *Goosebumps* series, House of Shivers, debuted in September 2023, with two more books published in 2024.

The *Goosebumps* series made R.L. Stine a worldwide publishing celebrity (and *Jeopardy!* answer). His other popular children's book series include Fear Street (recently revived as a feature film trilogy), The Garbage Pail Kids, Mostly Ghostly, The Nightmare Room, and Rotten School. Other titles include *It's the First Day of School ... Forever!*, *A Midsummer Night's Scream*, *Young Scrooge, Stinetinglers*, and three picture books, with Marc Brown—*The Little Shop of Monsters*, *Mary McScary*, and *Why Did the Monster Cross the Road*.

"To the Right Honourable William, Earl of Dartmouth" by Phillis Wheatley

Selected and with Commentary by Sumiko Saulson

Hail, happy day, when, smiling like the morn,
Fair Freedom rose New-England to adorn:
The northern clime beneath her genial ray,
Dartmouth, congratulates thy blissful sway:
Elate with hope her race no longer mourns,
Each soul expands, each grateful bosom burns,
While in thine hand with pleasure we behold
The silken reins, and Freedom's charms unfold.
Long lost to realms beneath the northern skies

She shines supreme, while hated faction dies:
Soon as appear'd the Goddess long desir'd,
Sick at the view, she languish'd and expir'd;
Thus from the splendors of the morning light
The owl in sadness seeks the caves of night.
No more, America, in mournful strain
Of wrongs, and grievance unredress'd complain,
No longer shalt thou dread the iron chain,
Which wanton Tyranny with lawless hand
Had made, and with it meant t' enslave the land.

Should you, my lord, while you peruse my song,
Wonder from whence my love of Freedom sprung,
Whence flow these wishes for the common good,
By feeling hearts alone best understood,
I, young in life, by seeming cruel fate
Was snatch'd from Afric's fancy'd happy seat:
What pangs excruciating must molest,

What sorrows labour in my parent's breast?
Steel'd was that soul and by no misery mov'd
That from a father seiz'd his babe belov'd:
Such, such my case. And can I then but pray
Others may never feel tyrannic sway?

For favours past, great Sir, our thanks are due,
And thee we ask thy favours to renew,
Since in thy pow'r, as in thy will before,
To sooth the griefs, which thou did'st once deplore.
May heav'nly grace the sacred sanction give
To all thy works, and thou for ever live
Not only on the wings of fleeting Fame,
Though praise immortal crowns the patriot's name,
But to conduct to heav'ns refulgent fane,
May fiery coursers sweep th' ethereal plain,
And bear thee upwards to that blest abode,
Where, like the prophet, thou shalt find thy God.

Observations

Phillis Wheatley was sold into slavery and brought to America as a child on the slave ship *Phillis*, which she was later named after. She was purchased by John Wheatley of Boston in 1761. The Wheatleys taught her to read and write, and she became renowned as a poet. She was the first English-speaking person of African descent to publish a book, *Poems on Various Subjects, Religious and Moral*, published in London in 1773. In it appears the poem "To the Right Honourable William, Earl of Darthmouth" written in 1772. In this moving piece, she implores the Earl of Dartmouth to bring an end to the tyrannies of slavery in the Colonies. It's final stanza vividly illustrates the evil that is slavery, focusing on the cruelty of stealing her as a child from her grieving parents' arms. In it, she describes the excruciating pangs that must molest and the sorrows that labor in her parent's breast.

Her poem stands out for its openly abolitionist views. Other openly abolitionist poetry by enslaved Africans in America would not be published for another fifty years, and while there were other enslaved poets, they were largely restricted to pious offerings. In fact, fellow enslaved Black poet Jupiter Hammon, a religious poet out of New York, and the first Black poet published in America, back in 1760, a year before Ms. Wheatley was abducted as a child from Africa, clapped back at her poem. In his response piece "An Address to Miss Phillis Wheatley," 1778, he speaks to Phillis Wheatley as though she were a wayward youth that ought to become more pious and godly and thank Jesus Christ that she was delivered from a "dark abode" (Africa), did not die on the slave ship, and was granted such freedoms and liberty in her life.

Phillis Wheatley did not see things that way, and her lines "I, young in life, by seeming cruel fate Was snatch'd from Afric's fancy'd happy seat" make clear her grief at being kidnapped from her parents and stolen away from the place of her birth in Africa. None of us can deny that slavery was an evil institution, and perhaps one of the most insidious forms of darkness was the perpetual censorship that forced the enslaved to put a happy face onto all their communications about the evils of it and to praise their oppressors even while writing works of protest.

About Sumiko Saulson

Sumiko Saulson is a Bram Stoker-nominated poet for their 2022 collection *The Rat King: A Book of Dark Poetry* (Dooky Zines), and an award-winning author of Afrosurrealist and multicultural sci-fi and horror whose latest novel *Happiness and Other Diseases* is available on Mocha Memoirs Press. She is the winner of the Horror Writers Association Scholarship from Hell (2016), BCC Voice "Reframing the Other" contest (2017), Mixy Award (2017), Afrosurrealist Writer Award (2018), Horror Writers Association Diversity Grant (2020), Horror Writers Association Richard Laymon Presidents Award (2021), and the Ladies of Horror Fiction Readers Choice Award (2021).

Sumiko has an Associates of Arts in English from Berkeley City College, writes a column called "Writing While Black" for the *San Francisco Bay View National Black Newspaper*, is the host of the SOMA Leather and LGBT Cultural District's "Erotic Storytelling Hour," and teaches courses at the Speculative Fiction Academy. Find her online at SumikoSaulson.com.

"Hymn to Pan" by John Keats
Selected and with Commentary by Jeffrey J. Mariotte

"O thou, whose mighty palace roof doth hang
From jagged trunks, and overshadoweth
Eternal whispers, glooms, the birth, life, death
Of unseen flowers in heavy peacefulness;
Who lov'st to see the hamadryads dress
Their ruffled locks where meeting hazels darken;
And through whole solemn hours dost sit, and hearken
The dreary melody of bedded reeds—
In desolate places, where dank moisture breeds
The pipy hemlock to strange overgrowth;
Bethinking thee, how melancholy loth
Thou wast to lose fair Syrinx—do thou now,
By thy love's milky brow!
By all the trembling mazes that she ran,
Hear us, great Pan!

"O thou, for whose soul-soothing quiet, turtles
Passion their voices cooingly 'mong myrtles,
What time thou wanderest at eventide
Through sunny meadows, that outskirt the side
Of thine enmossed realms: O thou, to whom
Broad leaved fig trees even now foredoom
Their ripen'd fruitage; yellow girted bees
Their golden honeycombs; our village leas
Their fairest blossom'd beans and poppied corn;
The chuckling linnet its five young unborn,
To sing for thee; low creeping strawberries
Their summer coolness; pent up butterflies

Their freckled wings; yea, the fresh budding year
All its completions—be quickly near,
By every wind that nods the mountain pine,
O forester divine!

"Thou, to whom every faun and satyr flies
For willing service; whether to surprise
The squatted hare while in half sleeping fit;
Or upward ragged precipices flit
To save poor lambkins from the eagle's maw;
Or by mysterious enticement draw
Bewildered shepherd to their path again;
Or to tread breathless round the frothy main,
And gather up all fancifullest shells
For thee to tumble into Naiads' cells,
And, being hidden, laugh at their out-peeping;
Or to delight thee with fantastic leaping,
The while they pelt each other on the crown
With silvery oak apples, and fir cones brown—
By all the echoes that about thee ring,
Hear us, O satyr king!

"O Hearkener to the loud clapping shears,
While ever and anon to his shorn peers
A ram goes bleating: Winder of the horn,
When snouted wild-boars routing tender corn
Anger our huntsmen: breather round our farms,
To keep off mildews, and all weather harms.
Strange ministrant of undescribed sounds,
That come a swooning over hollow grounds,
And wither drearily on barren moors:
Dread opener of the mysterious doors
Leading to universal knowledge—see,
Great son of Dryope,
The many that are come to pay their vows
With leaves about their brows!

"Be still the unimaginable lodge
For solitary thinkings; such as dodge
Conception to the very bourne of heaven,
Then leave the naked brain: be still the leaven,
That spreading in this dull and clodded earth
Gives it a touch ethereal—a new birth:
Be still a symbol of immensity;
A firmament reflected in a sea;

An element filling the space between,
An unknown—but no more: we humbly screen
With uplift hands our foreheads, lowly bending,
And giving out a shout most heaven rending,
Conjure thee to receive our humble Paean,
Upon thy Mount Lycean!"

OBSERVATIONS

The Great God Pan was a figure of uncertain origin and abilities, even to the ancient Greeks who worshipped him. He was said by some to be the oldest of the Greek gods, a teacher to Zeus. Other stories claim that Pan was the son of Hermes or Apollo. Part goat and part human, the god of forests and fields loved nature, music, dancing, and women.

John Keats, like other poets in the Romantic tradition, was drawn to nature, which became a dominant theme in his work. One of the acknowledged masterpieces of his brief career (Keats was published for only four years before dying of tuberculosis) was *Endymion*, of which "Hymn to Pan" is a part. Keats, longing for the imagined beauty and splendor that ancient Greece represents, tries to summon Pan. The contrast between the unspoiled nature that Pan represents with "this dull and clodded earth" shows the intensity of his desire.

Plutarch tells us, in one of the most specific tales of a Greek god's demise, that Pan is dead. He will not answer our summons. And the glory that was ancient Greece has faded, leaving us to "wither drearily on barren moors."

ABOUT JEFFREY J. MARIOTTE

Jeffrey J. Mariotte is the multiple-genre, multiple-award-winning author of more than sixty novels, dozens of short stories, and nearly two hundred comic books and graphic novels, among other things. He has worked in virtually every aspect of the book business as a bookstore manager and owner, VP of marketing, editor, and consultant for various publishing companies. When he's not writing, reading, or editing something, he's probably out enjoying the desert landscape around the Arizona home he shares with his family and dog and cats. Find him online at jeffmariotte.com.

"I DIED FOR BEAUTY" BY EMILY DICKINSON

SELECTED AND WITH COMMENTARY BY JANE YOLEN

POEM #449

I died for Beauty—but was scarce
Adjusted in the Tomb
When one who died for Truth was lain
In an adjoining room—

He questioned softly "Why I failed"?
"For Beauty—," I replied—
"And I—for Truth—Themself are One—
We Brethren are," he said—

And so, as Kinsmen, met—a Night—
We talked between the Rooms—
Until the Moss had reached our lips—
And covered up—Our names—

OBSERVATIONS

This is only one of many odd/weird death poems Dickinson wrote, with her own bizarre punctuation. A poem that hints at the reasons for each death without actually spelling either one out. Does dying for beauty mean someone's husband or wife or ex or a stalker murdered them? Or had they written something truthful or slighting—a poem, or song perhaps—that led to the death? Or does the poem refer to fact, fiction, or perhaps something even a bit more exotic?

And as for the truth the other newly dead person refers to—is it a personal truth, a religious truth, philosophical truth—or perhaps this person died for killing the other one? In fact, we the readers can only surmise but never know, because all too soon, the poet tells us, both mouths are shut forever by the moss of death. And unless Dickinson herself has written another poem that discloses what she knows—and I have not found that poem in her over 1,700 poems—it will remain both beautiful and sad, odd, and secret for all time.

About Jane Yolen

Jane Yolen is the author of over 450 books and is still writing. She has won multiple writing awards, including World Fantasy, Nebula Awards, Jewish Book Awards, SCBWI awards, and Catholic Library Medal. Her book *Owl Moon* won the Caldecott, and her *How Do Dinosaurs* books have sold over twenty-four million copies worldwide. She has six honorary doctorates from New England colleges and universities, was on the SCBWI board for forty-five years, and was the second woman ever to be president of the Science Fiction and Fantasy Writers of America.

"I felt a Funeral, in my Brain"
by Emily Dickinson
Selected and with Commentary
by John Russo

Poem #340

I felt a Funeral in my Brain,
And Mourners, to and fro,
Kept treading—treading—till it seemed
That Sense was breaking through—

And when they all were seated,
A Service like a Drum—
Kept beating—beating—till I thought
My mind was going numb—

And then I heard them lift a Box,
And creak across my Soul
With those same Boots of Lead, again,
Then Space—began to toll,

As all the Heavens were a Bell,
And Being but an Ear,
And I, and Silence, some strange Race,
Wrecked, solitary, here—

And then a Plank in Reason broke,
And I dropped down, and down—
And hit a World, at every plunge,
And finished knowing—then—

Observations

When I first heard of Emily Dickinson, as a sophomore English Education major at West Virginia University, her poems about death made a strong impression on me. Several lines from "The Bustle in a House" stayed in my mind from age nineteen onward: "The Bustle in a House, The Morning after Death," and "The Sweeping up the Heart, And putting Love away."

I cannot so easily recall specific lines from "I felt a Funeral, in my Brain," yet it has had a powerful influence upon me. It seems that Ms. Dickinson was terrified by a feeling that her brain was slipping away from her and that it was readying itself for its own funeral. Someone has commented that "the funeral" is not for her physical body but instead is for her mind. Perhaps it exemplifies the losing of the sense of self, losing sanity.

What could be more terrifying? It happens to victims of Alzheimer's.

This makes me wonder if Emily Dickinson might have been in the early stages of dementia when she wrote this poem. But, of course, she often wrote about death, and perhaps that is not so surprising, considering that she lived in an age with a very high mortality rate, and many, many death scenes played out in homes. It has also been conjectured that her melancholy aspect was due to her withdrawal, her reclusiveness, and her lack of romantic love. Agoraphobia? Again, one has to wonder.

As a child I had recurrent nightmares incited by the very first burial that I attended, along with my parents. The wife of one of my father's coworkers had died, and this was explained to me, even though, at six years old, I didn't understand what death was. But I saw her in her casket, and I saw the casket lowered into her grave, and the images that recurred in my nightmares were of her body falling through the bottom of the casket and into the earthen hole.

About John Russo

With forty books published internationally and nineteen feature movies in worldwide distribution, John Russo has been called a "living legend." He began by coauthoring the screenplay for *Night of the Living Dead*, which has become recognized as a "horror classic." His three books on the art and craft of moviemaking have become bibles of independent production, and one of them, *Scare Tactics*, won a national award for Superior Nonfiction. Quentin Tarantino and many other noted filmmakers have stated that Russo's books helped them launch their careers.

John Russo wants people to know he's "just a nice guy who likes to scare people"—and he's done it with novels and films such as *Return of the Living Dead*, *Midnight*, *The Majorettes*, *The Awakening*, *Heartstopper*, and *My Uncle John is a Zombie*. He has had a long, rewarding career, and he shows no signs of slowing down. One of his best novels, *Dealey Plaza*, dealing with the epidemic of gun violence in America, was published to great acclaim by Burning Bulb Publishing. And a series of new novels that he wrote during Covid has been brought out by Wolfpack Publishing and all have gotten four- and five-star reviews. His screenplay, *The Night They Came Home* is a Western horror story based on true events and is currently in production in California.

His popularity among genre fans remains at a high pitch. He appears at many movie conventions each year as a featured guest, and hundreds of attendees come to his tables or to the bar to share drinks, jokes, and serious conversation.

"I Have a Dead Friend"
by José Martí
Selected and with Commentary by Gaby Triana

(Verse VIII)

I have a dead friend who lately
Has begun to visit me:
My friend sits down and sings to me,
Sings to me so dolefully.

"Upon the double-winged bird's back
I am rowing through skies of blue:
One of the bird's wings is black,
The other, gold of Cariboo."

"The heart's a madman that abhors
One color as one too few:
Either its love is two colors,
Or else it is not love's hue."

"There's a madwoman more savage
Than is the unhappy heart:
She that sucks the blood in rage,
And then a-laughing would start."

"A heart that has lost forever
The steadfast anchor of home,
Sails like a ship in foul weather,
And knows not to go or come."

If his anguish should betray him,

The dead man will curse and weep:
I pat his skull and I lay him,
Lay the dead man down to sleep.

Yo Tengo un Amigo Muerto ... (Verso VIII)

Yo tengo un amigo muerto
Que suele venirme a ver:
Mi amigo se sienta, y canta;
Canta en voz que ha de doler.

"En un ave de dos alas
"Bogo por el cielo azul:
"Un ala del ave es negra,
"Otra de oro Caribú.

"El corazón es un loco
"Que no sabe de un color:
"O es su amor de dos colores,
"O dice que no es amor.

"Hay una loca más fiera
"Que el corazón infeliz:
"La que le chupó la sangre
"Y se echó luego a reír.

"Corazón que lleva rota
"El ancla fiel del hogar,
"Va como barca perdida,
"Que no sabe a dónde va."

En cuanto llega a esta angustia
Rompe el muerto a maldecir:
Le amanso el cráneo: lo acuesto:
Acuesto al muerto a dormir.

OBSERVATIONS

It's difficult to come from Caribbean heritage and never have heard of nationalist, journalist, essayist, poet, philosopher, social activist, and all-around literary hero of Latin America, José Martí. The man was a Cuban influencer, a fighter for Cuban independence from Spain, and you'd be hard-pressed to find an American of Cuban descent who wasn't raised on

José Martí poems as a child. Same way we grew up on rumbas, pastelitos, and baseball, Martí's "versos sencillos" (simple verses) were like Mother Goose rhymes for me, as my maternal grandmother, a professor of Spanish literature, recited one almost every morning as the day's icebreaker.

While Martí's poems were usually of a sociopolitical nature, this particular one always struck me as different with its more somber, reflective tone. Of course, the English version has been translated, and translations will vary, but all his writings were very simple, allowing themes to speak for themselves. What has always fascinated me about "Yo Tengo Un Amigo Muerto" is the theme of duality. Life is sweet, but it's also full of pain. Love manifests as a bird in flight but also as a vampire who drains your heart of lifeforce. One can express savagery but humor at the same time. One can be a sociopolitical commentator but also a poet of dark themes, all in the same breath. We are dual-sided beings, but it's usually our shadow side, the more psychologically complex side, that's more interesting, because it's the side that hinges on madness. What I love the most is that it's the narrator's dead friend singing these verses to him, because only a dead man who's been to the other side can truly know duality, and once you've seen it, you'll never be the same again.

About Gaby Triana

Gaby Triana is the Cuban American author of twenty-five books for adults and teens, including *Moon Child, Island of Bones, River of Ghosts, City of Spells, Wake the Hollow, Cubanita,* and *Summer of Yesterday.* Her short stories have appeared in *Classic Monsters Unleashed, A Tribute to Alvin Schwartz's Scary Stories to Tell in the Dark, A Conjuring for All Seasons, Novus Monstrum,* and *Weird Tales Magazine.* She has coauthored ghost hunters Sam & Colby's horror novel, *Paradise Island,* and edited the ghost anthology series, *Literally Dead (Tales of Halloween Hauntings; Tales of Holiday Hauntings).* As a ghostwriter, Gaby has penned more than fifty plus novels for bestselling authors in every genre. Her own books have won the International Reading Association Teen Choice Award, American Library Association Best Paperback, and Hispanic Magazine's Good Reads Awards, and she writes under several pen names, including Gabrielle Keyes for her paranormal women's fiction. She lives in Miami with her family and the four-legged creatures they serve.

"I Used to Be Invincible"
by Weston Ochse

Selected and with Commentary by Yvonne Navarro

(1965 - 2023)

The road wandered lonely along
the old path I walked to school when
I used to be invincible.

As always, I stopped the car and
trudged over to the ditch,
screams and pleas fresh in my ears
from my ten-year-old face
crushed and cracked like red and
gold autumn leaves renewed in the mulch
of youthful happiness

I had been proud that day
the blood flashing through my veins
no redneck boy would master me
even if they were like the cloying kudzu
smothering and devouring my dreams

I used to be invincible
until I was shown the face of rage
and the frowning emptiness of understanding,
and the inside of a hospital where my pain
translated to lights and beeps of machines
that didn't like invincible things.

Observations

My husband Weston Ochse always thought he was invincible. Over the years of our marriage, I have to admit that unconsciously I gradually began to believe the same thing. Eventually that would be both our undoing, because when he became ill, we assumed that of course he would get better ... but he didn't.

I first read this poem after he passed away. I came away believing that it was about his many lengthy stays in the hospital during his failing health. But as I read and reread it, I realized it was not about the present. It was about the past, an incident in his childhood when he went up against an older and much bigger kid in his class. The confrontation left him lying on the side of the Tennessee road, broken and bleeding, where his mother eventually found him and took him to the emergency room.

To me it seems like a fortune told, a glimpse into a future that would ultimately end in the same heartbreaking manner: in a hospital room filled with beeping machines that didn't care that he was invincible.

About Yvonne Navarro

Yvonne Navarro is an award-winning author of twenty-four published novels and a lot of short stories, articles, and a reference dictionary. She writes in a wide variety of genres but favors horror or dark fantasy. She lives in Tucson, Arizona, and is the heartbroken widow of author Weston Ochse.

"If We Must Die"
by Claude McKay
Selected and with Commentary
by Harold Perrineau

If we must die, let it not be like hogs
Hunted and penned in an inglorious spot,
While round us bark the mad and hungry dogs,
Making their mock at our accursèd lot.
If we must die, O let us nobly die,
So that our precious blood may not be shed
In vain; then even the monsters we defy
Shall be constrained to honor us though dead!
O kinsmen! we must meet the common foe!
Though far outnumbered let us show us brave,
And for their thousand blows deal one death-blow!
What though before us lies the open grave?
Like men we'll face the murderous, cowardly pack,
Pressed to the wall, dying, but fighting back!

Observations

"If We Must Die" by Claude McKay is one of my favorite poems, not only because on the face of it it's a poem of resistance (resistance is something many people respond to), but this form of resistance is felt on so many different levels.

The poem is written in a very culturally European form, which means that lessons taught by the oppressor were learned extremely well by the oppressed. Therefore, when the poem is read by anyone from the dominant culture it is fully understood by them. At the same time, it expresses the unique point of the oppressed people for whom the poem was written, making the poem uniquely theirs. In this way the poem becomes a self-defining cry for people who were often defined by others.

About Harold Perrineau

Harold Perrineau is an award-winning actor and producer who has made a name for himself gracing the big and small screen. His vast feature film career began with his breakout role as Mercutio, opposite Leonardo DiCaprio in Baz Luhrmann's stylized retelling of the Shakespeare tragedy *Romeo & Juliet*. Harold also starred in Dave Mamet's *The Edge*, The Wachowski's *The Matrix Trilogy*, Kathryn Bigelow's Oscar-nominated *Zero Dark Thirty*, and Paul Aster's *Smoke*, for which he received an Independent Spirit Award nomination, for Best Supporting Actor. After starring in in *Oz* on HBO and as Michael Dawson on *Lost*, he can now be seen in the MGM+ breakout hit *From*.

"In Flanders Fields" by John McCrae

Selected and with Commentary by Charlaine Harris

In Flanders fields the poppies blow
Between the crosses, row on row,
That mark our place; and in the sky
The larks, still bravely singing, fly
Scarce heard amid the guns below.

We are the Dead. Short days ago
We lived, felt dawn, saw sunset glow,
Loved and were loved, and now we lie,
In Flanders fields.

Take up our quarrel with the foe:
To you from failing hands we throw
The torch; be yours to hold it high.
If ye break faith with us who die
We shall not sleep, though poppies grow
In Flanders fields.

Observations

"In Flanders Fields" first appeared anonymously in 1915 but was published in an anthology of McCrae's poetry after his death in 1918. I have read this poem now and again through the years, and I always find something different to think about with each iteration. It's a very visual poem, and I can see the field of poppies, with wind whispering over them, making the flowers toss their heads. Underneath this beauty lies the bones of the soldiers who died: and the horror lies in the fact that over a million men were wounded, died, or went missing in this area of Belgium over the four years of WWI.

John McCrae was a Canadian, and a physician as well as a soldier. By the time he became drawn into World War I, he was a middle-aged man. Though he admitted in a letter to a friend that he was afraid, he was determined to do his duty. McCrae was incensed to be taken from his artillery group to serve as a doctor. He treated men in hastily dug trenches, under terrible conditions. During his service in France, McCrae died of pneumonia and was buried there. "In Flanders Fields" was widely used as a recruiting tool, which McCrae heartily approved.

The frightening aspect of this poem lies in its exhortation from the dead to the living. "If ye break faith with us who die ... We shall not sleep." All those dead soldiers, lying under the poppies forever ... will be wakeful in death, if the living do not hold high the torch. Inevitably, those who take up this torch will lie under the same sod. This is noble, grisly, and horrible, all at the same time.

About Charlaine Harris

Charlaine Harris, whose career has spanned over four decades, writes conventional mysteries, urban fantasy, and science fiction. A *New York Times* bestseller, she has sold over thirty million books, and hopes to sell more. Charlaine is a true daughter of the south, born in Mississippi and now living in Texas. She is the wife of one, mother of three, and grandmother of two. A graduate of Rhodes College, Charlaine enjoys reading more than anything else in the world, though baking comes in a close second. She loves having a dog in the house, and she loves her many friends.

"IN JUST" BY E.E. CUMMINGS
SELECTED AND WITH COMMENTARY BY SHANE BLACK

in Just—
springwhen the world is mud—
luscious the little
lame balloonman

whistles farand wee

and eddieandbill come
running from marbles and
piracies and it's
spring

when the world is puddle-wonderful
the queer
old balloonman whistles
farandwee
and bettyandisbel come dancing

from hop-scotch and jump-rope and

it's
spring
and
    the
        goat-footed
balloonMan whistles
far

and
wee

Observations

One reason I took to screenplays was the precision: every word counts. There is perhaps no finer (nor creepier) example of this than e.e. cummings "in Just-" which I encountered in AP English. The poem recalls the Fall From Heaven, in which Lucifer is lamed by a lightning bolt to his foot—hence: the queer little balloonman, left "goat-footed" and lame ... whistling on a corner, plying his offerings—causing local kids to drop what they're doing one "puddle-wonderful" spring and come running, at his beck and call.

I grew up in small-town, suburban America, and subsequent to this poem I discovered *Something Wicked This Way Comes*, by Ray Bradbury. The idea of Evil, glimpsed in passing throughout our childhood—always cloaked in circus raiments, balloons, candy, beckoning tent shows—is always chilling; a world where the parents aren't around to save us, and children must stand (alone) against an evil to which numb adults are mercifully oblivious—hypnotized by their own shame at having failed. Later, I would trot out my own take on this (with Fred Dekker) in *The Monster Squad*, a 1987 box-office bomb that is now a long-running midnight movie.

About Shane Black

Shane Black is a filmmaker and actor who has written such films as *Lethal Weapon*, *The Monster Squad*, *The Last Boy Scout*, *Last Action Hero*, and *The Long Kiss Goodnight*. He is also known as the original creator of the Lethal Weapon franchise. As an actor, Black is best known for his role as Rick Hawkins in *Predator*. He made his directorial debut with the film *Kiss Kiss Bang Bang* in 2005. Black went on to write and direct *Iron Man 3* and *The Nice Guys*, among others. In 2005, he received the Best Original Screenplay award for *Kiss Kiss Bang Bang* from the San Diego Film Critics Association. Black received the Distinguished Screenwriter Award from the Austin Film Festival in 2006.

"In the Desert" by Stephen Crane

Selected and with Commentary by Cullen Bunn

In the desert
I saw a creature, naked, bestial,
Who, squatting upon the ground,
Held his heart in his hands,
And ate of it.
I said, "Is it good, friend?"
"It is bitter—bitter," he answered;
"But I like it
"Because it is bitter,
"And because it is my heart."

Observations

I'm not sure there has ever been a poem that has stuck with me—haunted me—the way this short little number has. When I first stumbled upon it in an old college textbook I picked up at a garage sale. I was stunned by the creature's loneliness and self-destructive nature.

In one way or another, the heart-eating creature has shown up in much of my work. The Skinless Boy in *Harrow County*? He's this creature. The soul-collecting Harvester in *The Damned*? He shares DNA with the poem's creature. When a character in one of my stories takes a selfish, egocentric, self-destructive action, something that demonstrates a degree of both self-love *and* self-loathing, the creature, blood and bits of bitter heart on its chin, is looking over their shoulder.

And, so, maybe the creature is me.

Maybe that's why the poem resonated with me the way it did. When I read the poem—and especially during the dark time in my life when I first discovered it—I was in the desert, I was the narrator, and I was the creature.

And I still like the bitter taste of my heart.

About Cullen Bunn

Cullen Bunn is a writer of comic books, prose, film, and TV. He has written stories for some of the most well-known characters in the world. His work for Marvel and DC includes titles such as *Uncanny X-Men, X-Men Blue, Deadpool Kills the Marvel Universe, Magento,* and *Sinestro*. His creator-owned work includes *The Sixth Gun, Harrow County, The Empty Man, Bone Parish, Basilisk,* and many others. His prose horror novel *Bones of our Stars, Blood of our World* comes out from Gallery Books in 2025. His website is cullenbunn.com.

"Terror Management and the Worm at the Core"
by Travis Langley
An Essay on Darkness

You wonder what lurks in those shadows outside your window, down the hall, in the corners, or beneath your bed. Dangers exist, you know that. Vigilance helps you survive by alerting you to risks, but it can also keep you trapped. Excessive preoccupation with potential danger, *hypervigilance*, interferes with truly living life. At the other extreme, insufficient concern or responsiveness to risk, *hypovigilance*, can lead you right into the monster's jaws. To help you find and walk the ever-shifting line in between, you mentally and emotionally rehearse your fear responses in safer settings and times.

Existential psychologists suggest that human beings' awareness of our fleeting mortality will motivate most choices we make and things we do. We want to make life worth living in the moment, to keep ourselves alive, and to find ways we might continue to exist beyond physical life. For psychologist Viktor Frankl, who later spread existential psychology throughout the world, many of his ideas about this grew out of his years surviving the horrors of Auschwitz and other concentration camps. To keep ourselves going, we want our fear and pain to matter. We dread the idea of suffering for nothing. Frankl concluded that we do not simply try to find meaning in life. Instead, to survive and even thrive, we feel driven to make it mean something.

In a modern, more scientifically based spin, *terror management theory* suggests that the mental conflict over desiring life versus knowing death's inevitably creates the terror that we continually work to control. In this line of thought, death anxiety not only makes us seek to extend life and hope for afterlife, but it also guides and empowers nearly everything we do: We want the symbolic immortality of leaving an impression upon others, having an impact in the world, and knowing it will matter that we were here. Terror management theorists say the terror never really leaves us; therefore, we do what we can to work with it rather than drown in it. More than a hundred years ago, psychologist William James paved the way for Frankl and the rest when he called the knowledge that we must die "the worm at the core" of human existence.

When you read a horror novel, watch a spooky movie, or tell your own scary story, you are making an affirmative choice: You will face that worm, not hide from it or flee. You will practice your hereditary survival response in manageable ways so that you might strengthen yourself and overcome the worm's power to hurt you: You exercise to exorcise. It's just as true when you follow uncanny poetry through one eerie line after another. Every poem and essay in this volume helps you work with the worm rather than against it, because even the freest, most unstructured verse transforms abstract terror into concrete text.

Instead of letting terror crush you, you read or write the spooky verse because it lets you mount the worm and maybe nudge it to take you where you need. You do not simply walk that tortuous line between the extremes of vigilance. You ride over it.

About Travis Langley

Travis Langley, PhD, professor of psychology, is best known as author of the book *Batman and Psychology: A Dark and Stormy Knight*. He serves as editor, lead writer, and head nerd of the herd for the Popular Culture Psychology book series. His anthologies examine *Supernatural*, *Stranger Things*, *Game of Thrones*, *The Walking Dead*, *The Handmaid's Tale*, and more to explore real human nature through modern media examples. *The Wall Street Journal*, *The New York Times*, *LA Times*, *The Saturday Evening Post*, CNN, MTV, and hundreds of other outlets have interviewed him and covered his work. Find him on social media as @Superherologist or @DrTravisLangley.

"Jessie Cameron" by Christina Rossetti
Selected and with Commentary by Dennis Tafoya

"Jessie, Jessie Cameron,
Hear me but this once," quoth he.
"Good luck go with you, neighbor's son,
But I'm no mate for you," quoth she.
Day was verging toward the night
There beside the moaning sea,
Dimness overtook the light
There where the breakers be.
"O Jessie, Jessie Cameron,
I have loved you long and true."—
"Good luck go with you, neighbor's son,
But I'm no mate for you."

She was a careless, fearless girl,
And made her answer plain;
Outspoken she to earl or churl,
Kindhearted in the main,
But somewhat heedless with her tongue,
And apt at causing pain;
A mirthful maiden she and young,
Most fair for bliss or bane.
"O, long ago I told you so,
I tell you so to-day:
Go you your way, and let me go
Just my own free way."

The sea swept in with moan and foam
Quickening the stretch of sand;

They stood almost in sight of home;
He strove to take her hand.
"Oh, can't you take your answer then,
And won't you understand?
For me you're not the man of men,
I've other plans are planned.
You're good for Madge, or good for Cis,
Or good for Kate, may be:
But what's to me the good of this
While you're not good for me?"

They stood together on the beach,
They two alone,
And louder waxed his urgent speech,
His patience almost gone:
"O, say but one kind word to me,
Jessie, Jessie Cameron."—
"I'd be too proud to beg," quoth she,
And pride was in her tone.
And pride was in her lifted head,
And in her angry eye,
And in her foot, which might have fled,
But would not fly.

Some say that he had gypsy blood,
That in his heart was guile:
Yet he had gone through fire and flood
Only to win her smile.
Some say his grandam was a witch,
A black witch from beyond the Nile,
Who kept an image in a niche
And talked with it the while.
And by her hut far down the lane
Some say they would not pass at night,
Lest they should hear an unked strain
Or see an unked sight.

Alas, for Jessie Cameron!—
The sea crept moaning, moaning nigher:
She should have hastened to be gone,—
The sea swept higher, breaking by her:
She should have hastened to her home
While yet the west was flushed with fire,
But now her feet are in the foam,
The sea-foam, sweeping higher.

O mother, linger at your door,
And light your lamp to make it plain;
But Jessie she comes home no more,
No more again.

They stood together on the strand,
They only, each by each;
Home, her home, was close at hand,
Utterly out of reach.
Her mother in the chimney nook
Heard a startled sea-gull screech,
But never turned her head to look
Towards the darkening beach:
Neighbors here and neighbors there
Heard one scream, as if a bird
Shrilly screaming cleft the air:—
That was all they heard.

Jessie she comes home no more,
Comes home never;
Her lover's step sounds at his door
No more forever.
And boats may search upon the sea
And search along the river,
But none know where the bodies be:
Sea-winds that shiver,
Sea-birds that breast the blast,
Sea-waves swelling,
Keep the secret first and last
Of their dwelling.

Whether the tide so hemmed them round
With its pitiless flow,
That when they would have gone they found
No way to go;
Whether she scorned him to the last
With words flung to and fro,
Or clung to him when hope was past,
None will ever know:
Whether he helped or hindered her,
Threw up his life or lost it well,
The troubled sea, for all its stir,
Finds no voice to tell.

Only watchers by the dying

Have thought they heard one pray,
Wordless, urgent; and replying
One seem to say him nay:
And watchers by the dead have heard
A windy swell from miles away,
With sobs and screams, but not a word
Distinct for them to say:
And watchers out at sea have caught
Glimpse of a pale gleam here or there,
Come and gone as quick as thought,
Which might be hand or hair.

OBSERVATIONS

I like to think of "Jessie Cameron" as a crime story in ten stanzas, about a proud young woman whose attempts to reject an unwanted suitor ends in a mysterious death in a rising tide. Was it an accident? Or murder and suicide? As readers, we're left to the mercies of unreliable neighbors whose speculations run to racism, dark magic, and the pride of a "careless, fearless girl." Rossetti's poem, with its eponymous title and dire speculations about the fate and motivations of the couple on the "darkened beach," succeeds in calling back to the traditions of the woeful murder ballad and forward to our never-ending engagement with details of actual crimes. It's not hard to imagine Jessie Cameron's final hours being the subject of a multi-part podcast, including the perceptions of gossipy neighbors who wondered about the young man's gypsy blood and the pride in Jessie's "lifted head and angry eye."

The poem, like the best crime fiction, conjures both the "unked"—the unknown—and the familiar terrors that haunt our everyday lives. Rosetti, living in a time when English coverture law held that a married woman could own no property, in fact had no independent legal identity, knew intimately the struggle to remain her own person. Here she affirms what any woman in any age might recognize—that in Jessie Cameron's battle to go "just my own free way" the stakes could be life and death.

About Dennis Tafoya

Dennis Tafoya lives near Philadelphia and is the author of three crime novels set in and around the city, including *Dope Thief*, currently being filmed for Apple TV as *Sinking Spring*. His short stories have appeared in magazines and anthologies such as *Philadelphia Noir* and *Best American Mystery Stories*. His work has been nominated for multiple awards and optioned for film and television.

"On Joy and Sorrow" by Kahlil Gibran
Submitted and with Commentary by Lisa Diane Kastner

Chapter VIII

Then a woman said, "Speak to us of Joy and Sorrow."
And he answered:
Your joy is your sorrow unmasked.
And the selfsame well from which your laughter rises was oftentimes filled with your tears.
And how else can it be?
The deeper that sorrow carves into your being, the more joy you can contain.
Is not the cup that hold your wine the very cup that was burned in the potter's oven?
And is not the lute that soothes your spirit, the very wood that was hollowed with knives?
When you are joyous, look deep into your heart and you shall find it is only that which has given you sorrow that is giving you joy.
When you are sorrowful look again in your heart, and you shall see that in truth you are weeping for that which has been your delight.
Some of you say, "Joy is greater than sorrow," and others say, "Nay, sorrow is the greater."
But I say unto you, they are inseparable.
Together they come, and when one sits alone with you at your board, remember that the other is asleep upon your bed.
Verily you are suspended like scales between your sorrow and your joy.

Only when you are empty are you at standstill and balanced. When the treasure-keeper lifts you to weigh his gold and his silver, needs must your joy or your sorrow rise or fall.

OBSERVATIONS

Gibran evokes a truth that many of us experience and may not acknowledge—that some of our greatest moments are often rooted in pain, sadness, difficulty.

When I reflect on my life, I definitely see this truth. An example is that when I was twenty, I came home to find my house had been burned down. I still remember the moment in which something clicked inside me, and I thought "Now is the time."

ABOUT LISA DIANE KASTNER

Lisa Diane Kastner is the Founder of Running Wild, LLC, a content creation, distribution, and licensing company. Featured in *Forbes* and several other publications, she's been named to multiple "Best of"s. A writer and editor for more than twenty years, she has identified talent like Jamie Ford's *Hotel on the Corner of Bitter and Sweet*, Reuben "Tihi" Hayslett's *Dark Corners*, Suzanne Samples's *Frontal Matter: Glue Gone Wild*, Tori Eldridge's *Dance Among the Flames*, Shay Galloway's *The Valley of Sage and Juniper*, and many other authors whose works have been named groundbreaking in their respective genres as well as best of the year.

"Jubilate Agno" by Christopher Smart
Selected and with Commentary by Charlie Jane Anders

(an excerpt from "Jubilate Agno")

For I will consider my Cat Jeoffry.
For he is the servant of the Living God duly and daily serving him.
For at the first glance of the glory of God in the East he worships in his way.
For this is done by wreathing his body seven times round with elegant quickness.
For then he leaps up to catch the musk, which is the blessing of God upon his prayer.
For he rolls upon prank to work it in.
For having done duty and received blessing he begins to consider himself.
For this he performs in ten degrees.
For first he looks upon his forepaws to see if they are clean.
For secondly he kicks up behind to clear away there.
For thirdly he works it upon stretch with the forepaws extended.
For fourthly he sharpens his paws by wood.
For fifthly he washes himself.
For sixthly he rolls upon wash.
For seventhly he fleas himself, that he may not be interrupted upon the beat.
For eighthly he rubs himself against a post.
For ninthly he looks up for his instructions.
For tenthly he goes in quest of food.

For having consider'd God and himself he will consider his neighbour.
For if he meets another cat he will kiss her in kindness.
For when he takes his prey he plays with it to give it a chance.
For one mouse in seven escapes by his dallying.
For when his day's work is done his business more properly begins.
For he keeps the Lord's watch in the night against the adversary.
For he counteracts the powers of darkness by his electrical skin and glaring eyes.
For he counteracts the Devil, who is death, by brisking about the life.
For in his morning orisons he loves the sun and the sun loves him.
For he is of the tribe of Tiger.
For the Cherub Cat is a term of the Angel Tiger.
For he has the subtlety and hissing of a serpent, which in goodness he suppresses.
For he will not do destruction, if he is well-fed, neither will he spit without provocation.
For he purrs in thankfulness, when God tells him he's a good Cat.
For he is an instrument for the children to learn benevolence upon.
For every house is incomplete without him and a blessing is lacking in the spirit.
For the Lord commanded Moses concerning the cats at the departure of the Children of Israel from Egypt.
For every family had one cat at least in the bag.
For the English Cats are the best in Europe.
For he is the cleanest in the use of his forepaws of any quadruped.
For the dexterity of his defence is an instance of the love of God to him exceedingly.
For he is the quickest to his mark of any creature.
For he is tenacious of his point.
For he is a mixture of gravity and waggery.
For he knows that God is his Saviour.
For there is nothing sweeter than his peace when at rest.
For there is nothing brisker than his life when in motion.
For he is of the Lord's poor and so indeed is he called by benevolence perpetually—Poor Jeoffry! poor Jeoffry! the rat has bit thy throat.

For I bless the name of the Lord Jesus that Jeoffry is better.
For the divine spirit comes about his body to sustain it in complete cat.
For his tongue is exceeding pure so that it has in purity what it wants in music.
For he is docile and can learn certain things.
For he can set up with gravity which is patience upon approbation.
For he can fetch and carry, which is patience in employment.
For he can jump over a stick which is patience upon proof positive.
For he can spraggle upon waggle at the word of command.
For he can jump from an eminence into his master's bosom.
For he can catch the cork and toss it again.
For he is hated by the hypocrite and miser.
For the former is afraid of detection.
For the latter refuses the charge.
For he camels his back to bear the first notion of business.
For he is good to think on, if a man would express himself neatly.
For he made a great figure in Egypt for his signal services.
For he killed the Ichneumon-rat very pernicious by land.
For his ears are so acute that they sting again.
For from this proceeds the passing quickness of his attention.
For by stroking of him I have found out electricity.
For I perceived God's light about him both wax and fire.
For the Electrical fire is the spiritual substance, which God sends from heaven to sustain the bodies both of man and beast.
For God has blessed him in the variety of his movements.
For, tho he cannot fly, he is an excellent clamberer.
For his motions upon the face of the earth are more than any other quadruped.
For he can tread to all the measures upon the music.
For he can swim for life.
For he can creep.

Observations

"Jubilate Agno" by Christopher Smart is surely one of the most profound and potent works of verse ever written. Smart, languishing in an eighteenth-century mental institution, writes about God and about Nimrod the mighty hunter, but also about cats and mice, and many other topics. Immortalized by Benjamin Britten in one of the all-time great choral works, "Jubilate Agno" nevertheless deserves to be read on its own, for its ringing clarity and its strange quality of wistful joy. Smart was famous in the eighteenth century as a translator of the Roman poet Horace, whose writings about people's relationship with nature were often quoted at the time. And in his own writings, Smart sees nature as a window on the divine —especially the mice, who are creatures of great valor!

My favorite bit—probably everybody's favorite bit—is the description of Smart's beloved cat Jeoffry, who lived with him in St. Luke's Hospital. This is the best description of a cat's behavior that I've ever read: the wreathing around, the considering his own paws, the looking upward as if for instructions, the dallying with mice. It's pure magic, and utterly holy. I don't even believe in God, but reading Smart's description of Jeoffry makes me feel an irresistible connection to something huge and mysterious in the universe.

About Charlie Jane Anders

Charlie Jane Anders is the author of *The Prodigal Mother*, coming in 2025. Her work has appeared most recently in *Fourteen Days*, a collaborative novel edited by Margaret Atwood and Douglas Preston. She also wrote *Never Say You Can't Survive*, a book about using creative writing to get through hard times, and a short story collection, *Even Greater Mistakes: Stories*. Her young adult *Unstoppable* trilogy has been nominated for the Lodestar and Andre Norton Awards and has won two Locus Awards. She co-hosts the podcast *Our Opinions Are Correct*.

"La Belle Dame sans Merci"
by John Keats
Selected and with Commentary
by Melissa Marr

Ah, what can ail thee, wretched wight,
Alone and palely loitering;
The sedge is withered from the lake,
And no birds sing.

Ah, what can ail thee, wretched wight,
So haggard and so woe-begone?
The squirrel's granary is full,
And the harvest's done.

I see a lilly on thy brow,
With anguish moist and fever dew;
And on thy cheek a fading rose
Fast withereth too.

I met a lady in the meads
Full beautiful, a faery's child;
Her hair was long, her foot was light,
And her eyes were wild.

I set her on my pacing steed,
And nothing else saw all day long;
For sideways would she lean, and sing
A faery's song.

I made a garland for her head,
And bracelets too, and fragrant zone;

She looked at me as she did love,
And made sweet moan.

She found me roots of relish sweet,
And honey wild, and manna dew;
And sure in language strange she said,
I love thee true.

She took me to her elfin grot,
And there she gazed and sighed deep,
And there I shut her wild sad eyes—
So kissed to sleep.

And there we slumbered on the moss,
And there I dreamed, ah woe betide,
The latest dream I ever dreamed
On the cold hill side.

I saw pale kings, and princes too,
Pale warriors, death-pale were they all;
Who cried—"La belle Dame sans merci
Hath thee in thrall!"

I saw their starved lips in the gloam
With horrid warning gaped wide,
And I awoke, and found me here
On the cold hill side.

And this is why I sojourn here
Alone and palely loitering,
Though the sedge is withered from the lake,
And no birds sing.

OBSERVATIONS

Like many a genre-writer-to-be, I was always drawn to the arts that include the fantastic, the supernatural, or folklore. When I first read "La Belle Dame sans Merci" I read it literally. Keats was talking about a man who meets a faery. In fact, there are faeries who were reputed to loiter along rivers or streams, the *leanan sidhe* (fairy lover) or *gancanagh*. As a child who grew up *believing* in faeries in the wood behind my home, a child who was told that *bean sidhes* (spelled "banshee" in popular culture) lingered by "the old well" so I ought not go there if I wanted to live ... here was a poem from my schoolwork telling me the same thing. As a young person, I read this as a sort of validation of the things I was raised to think of as "rules." Here was a man who lived over a *century* before me, writing about someone ignoring my grandmother's rules!

As I grew older, I learned that this "wasting disease" might have been tuberculosis or even a sexually transmitted illness, and I became increasingly fascinated by the idea of one thing meaning many things at once—not in a "this is right" and "that is wrong" way, but in the way that a multiplicity of meanings could coexist. The revelations about this poem were both part of my transition from barefooted country girl to serious lit student to actual lit *teacher* to writer. And somewhere in the middle, I came to understand that it doesn't *matter* whether the knight kissed a faery or a woman with an illness (be it tuberculosis or an STI). What mattered was that sometimes we risk everything for a kiss ... and as a woman who started dating women back when tolerance was rare and lesbian relationships were illegal (and marriage was too!), I thought Keats continued to make a lot of sense on a different personal level. Not all literature has a timeless reach or even a deeply personal one, but for me "La Belle Dame sans Merci" has been one of the poems that has informed my journey both in my careers and my life.

About Melissa Marr

Melissa Marr writes fiction for adults, teens, and children. Her books have been translated into twenty-eight languages and been bestsellers domestically (*The New York Times*, *USA Today*, *The Wall Street Journal*, etc.) and internationally. She is best known for the Wicked Lovely series for teens and *Bunny Roo, I Love You* for young readers. She teaches occasionally for Southern New Hampshire University's MFA program. In her pre-writing life, she taught literature for North Carolina State University. Currently, she lives in Arizona with her wife and son.

"LE LÉTHÉ"
BY CHARLES BAUDELAIRE
SELECTED AND WITH COMMENTARY
BY DELILAH S. DAWSON

Come to my heart, you tiger I adore.
You sullen monster, cruel and speechless spirit;
Into the thickness of your heavy mane
I want to plunge my trembling fingers' grip.

I want to hide the throbbing of my head
In your perfume, under those petticoats,
And breathe the musky scent of our old love,
The fading fragrance of the dying rose.

I want to sleep! to sleep and not to live!
And in a sleep as sweet as death, to dream
Of spreading out my kisses without shame
On your smooth body, bright with copper sheen.

If I would swallow down my softened sobs
It must be in your bed's profound abyss -
Forgetfulness is moistening your breath,
Lethe itself runs smoothly in your kiss.

My destiny, from now on my delight,
Is to obey as one who has been sent
To guiltless martyrdom, when all the while
His passion fans the flames of his torment.

My lips will suck the cure for bitterness:
Oblivion, nepenthe has its start

In the bewitching teats of those hard breasts,
That never have been harbour of a heart.

Observations

I discovered Baudelaire in late high school, somewhere between my first heartbreak and my suicide attempt while studying abroad in France. I bought a paperback of *Les Fleurs du Mal*—*The Flowers of Evil*—to dogear and underline as its pages gently faded from fresh cream to the color of an old man's tobacco-stained teeth. I was fluent back then, fluent enough to watch *Tank Girl* in Toulouse and mostly understand it. "La Léthé" was my favorite poem, in part because I loved the first line: "Come to my heart, you tiger I adore."

I grew up in a house with domestic violence and alcoholism, both kept carefully hidden, and so I made a fortress of my heart to ensure I could never be hurt by outside forces. It was easier to think of myself as a cruel tiger than to face the fact that I didn't fully trust anyone, easier to be dark and mysterious and impenetrable than to show anyone my soft and vulnerable side. I, too, wanted to sleep and not to live, to sweetly dream of a life without shame. This poem was banned in 1857 for being offensive to public sensibilities, but what has always struck me is its sadness, its yearning. Whoever she was, this woman whose body wept oblivion, she had a heart, and she had a reason for keeping it hidden.

(Author's Note: I got better.)

About Delilah S. Dawson

Delilah S. Dawson is *The New York Times* bestselling author of *Star Wars Phasma*, as well as *It Will Only Hurt for a Moment, The Violence, Bloom, Guillotine, Mine, Camp Scare, Midnight at the Houdini, Servants of the Storm*, the Hit series, the Blud series, the Minecraft Mob Squad series, and the Shadow series, written as Lila Bowen. With Kevin Hearne, she writes the *Tales of Pell*. Delilah lives in Atlanta with her family and still knows a little French. Find her online at delilahsdawson.com and on social media @delilahsdawson.

"Mexican Poetry"
by Jose de Saltillo
Selected and with Commentary
by V. Castro

Hearken! From our Northern borders
Sounds Arista's bugle call;
On the banks of Rio Bravo,
Bursts the shell and ploughs the ball!

Ghastly hands in Tenochtitlan
Strike th' old Aztec battle drum;
Sharp of beak and strong of talon,
Lo, Mexitli's eagle come!

Coldly sleep our slaughtered brothers,
While above their hasty graves
Sounds of hurrying foot of rapine,
And the robber banner waves.

On they come, the mad invaders,
Like the fire before the wind;
Freedom's harvest field before them,
Slavery's blackened waste behind.

From the sellers of God's image—
From the trafficker's in Man—
Mother gracious, mother holy,
Shield thy dark browed Mexican!

Hearken! up the Rio Bravo,
Come the negro-catcher's shout!
Listen! 'tis the Yankees's hammer,

Forging human fetter's out.

Let the land we love be wasted,
Black with fire, and rough with graves;
Better far, for God and Freedom
Die at once, than die as slaves

We are few, and they are many,
Strong in arms and wealth and pride;
But the saints and holy angels
And man's heart on our side

Hark! From Ancient Tenochtitlan,
Sounds once more from the Aztec drums;
Not for conquest, not for vengeance,
But for freedom, faith and home.

Observations

I often write about identity and history as a native Texan and Mexican American woman. My entire existence is based upon the mixing of culture and races born from the Spanish invasion and conquest of what we now call Mexico. However, folklore and the power of storytelling did not die with those enslaved. The images of the past remained alive through generations. Later, Texas became a disputed land that became part of the US after much blood shed and war with Mexico.

This poem was included in a publication called *The Signal of Liberty*. Every Saturday, Foster and Dell published this magazine for the Michigan Anti-Slavery Society. Both Brown and Black folks endured real-life horror by others who sought to steal land and use them for forced labor.

This poem called to me because it's a soul's cry for freedom and help from the ancestors. Tenochtitlan was the center of Aztec power and the eagle with a snake its beak was the sign they saw when deciding to build their great pyramid that stood proud until destroyed by the Spanish. The writer called for that power to protect him and others because death is better than enslavement. Freedom to be who you are is priceless. This poem makes me feel so very sad, but grateful he endured living with signs that read, "No Dogs, No Mexicans, No Negros." I've been given the chance by my ancestors to do what they could not.

Tenochtitlan lives in me.

About V. Castro

V. Castro is a two-time Bram Stoker Award-nominated Mexican American writer from San Antonio, Texas, now residing in the UK. She writes horror, erotic horror, and science fiction. Her books include *The Haunting of Alejandra*, *Alien: Vasquez*, *Mestiza Blood*, *The Queen of the Cicadas*, *Out of Aztlan*, *Las Posadas*, *Dia de Los Slashers*, *Rebel Moon* (official film novelization), *Goddess of Filth*, and *Immortal Pleasures*. Find her online via Instagram and Twitter @vlatinalondon or vcastrostories.com. She can also be found on Blue Sky, Goodreads, and Amazon. TikTok@vcastrobooks.

"My Last Duchess"
by Robert Browning
Selected and with Commentary by Stephen Graham Jones

FERRARA

That's my last Duchess painted on the wall,
Looking as if she were alive. I call
That piece a wonder, now; Fra Pandolf's hands
Worked busily a day, and there she stands.

Will't please you sit and look at her? I said
"Fra Pandolf" by design, for never read
Strangers like you that pictured countenance,
The depth and passion of its earnest glance,

But to myself they turned (since none puts by
The curtain I have drawn for you, but I)
And seemed as they would ask me, if they durst,
How such a glance came there; so, not the first

Are you to turn and ask thus. Sir, 'twas not
Her husband's presence only, called that spot
Of joy into the Duchess' cheek; perhaps
Fra Pandolf chanced to say, "Her mantle laps

Over my lady's wrist too much," or "Paint
Must never hope to reproduce the faint
Half-flush that dies along her throat." Such stuff
Was courtesy, she thought, and cause enough

For calling up that spot of joy. She had

A heart—how shall I say?—too soon made glad,
Too easily impressed; she liked whate'er
She looked on, and her looks went everywhere.

Sir, 'twas all one! My favour at her breast,
The dropping of the daylight in the West,
The bough of cherries some officious fool
Broke in the orchard for her, the white mule

She rode with round the terrace—all and each
Would draw from her alike the approving speech,
Or blush, at least. She thanked men—good! but thanked
Somehow—I know not how—as if she ranked

My gift of a nine-hundred-years-old name
With anybody's gift. Who'd stoop to blame
This sort of trifling? Even had you skill
In speech—which I have not—to make your will

Quite clear to such an one, and say, "Just this
Or that in you disgusts me; here you miss,
Or there exceed the mark"—and if she let
Herself be lessoned so, nor plainly set

Her wits to yours, forsooth, and made excuse—
E'en then would be some stooping; and I choose
Never to stoop. Oh, sir, she smiled, no doubt,
Whene'er I passed her; but who passed without

Much the same smile? This grew; I gave commands;
Then all smiles stopped together. There she stands
As if alive. Will't please you rise? We'll meet
The company below, then. I repeat,

The Count your master's known munificence
Is ample warrant that no just pretense
Of mine for dowry will be disallowed;
Though his fair daughter's self, as I avowed

At starting, is my object. Nay, we'll go
Together down, sir. Notice Neptune, though,
Taming a sea-horse, thought a rarity,
Which Claus of Innsbruck cast in bronze for me!

Observations

Dramatic monologues don't get the attention they should. They have such potential, and it's all on display in this poem—originally titled "Italy," which results in such a different read—where a speaker is showing off a painting of his former wife to a party guest, but, just as in Brian Evenson's story *The Munich Window* (Altmann's Tongue, 1994), we slowly realize that the person telling this grand version of events is actually guilty of murder. While the dramatic monologue is often mistaken for second-person, as they both use "you," it's essentially different. It's more like a one-sided conversation we're privy to, where the person being spoken to doesn't get any of their lines onto the page; the person being spoken to is just "there," putatively listening—sort of a stand in for us, the reader, but different in that their presence provides a dramatic context, a scene. Here, Robert Browning's narrator, who is of the nobility (as the epigraph establishes), is pretty much showing off that he's gotten away with killing his wife, and the dramatic monologue is his list of reasons for killing her. Granted, he phrases it all elliptically, but you can hear him smirking between the lines. Each rhyming couplet indicts him further, yet he can't help himself; he's so entitled that he knows he's getting away with it.

Furthermore, as far as he's concerned, she deserved it, so he feels no guilt, and now keeps her portrait as a trophy on his wall, like the other pieces of art. The guy's evil, definitely, but the disturbing part of the poem is that, due to his station in life, we know he's never going to get punished. Worse, the party guest being told all this is surely in on the hush-hush "joke" of it all, which is to say: it's a class thing, this dispensing with troublesome wives. To be sure, Robert Browning is in no way supportive of this. Rather, this is his indictment of that behavior. Poetry's best when it's angry, and, here, for all the perceived humor, for all the attention to form, for all the indirectness, there's still a distinct anger bubbling just under the surface, that acts like these have happened, and that they keep happening.

About Stephen Graham Jones

Stephen Graham Jones is *The New York Times* bestselling author of some thirty novels and collections, and there's some novellas and comic books in there as well. Most recent are *The Angel of Indian Lake* and the ongoing *Earthdivers*. Up before too long is *I Was a Teenage Slasher* and *True Believers*. Stephen lives and teaches in Boulder, Colorado.

"Nathicana" by H.P. Lovecraft
Selected and with Commentary by Samantha Underhill

(published under the pseudonym, Albert Frederick Willie)

It was in the pale garden of Zaïs;
The mist-shrouded gardens of Zaïs,
Where blossoms the white nephalotë,
The redolent herald of midnight.
There slumber the still lakes of crystal,
And streamlets that flow without murm'ring;
Smooth streamlets from caverns of Kathos
Where brood the calm spirits of twilight.
And over the lakes and the streamlets
Are bridges of pure alabaster,
White bridges all cunningly carven
With figures of fairies and daemons.
Here glimmer strange suns and strange planets,
And strange is the crescent Banapis
That sets 'yond the ivy-grown ramparts
Where thickens the dust of the evening.
Here fall the white vapours of Yabon;
And here in the swirl of vapours
I saw the divine Nathicana;
The garlanded, white Nathicana;
The slender, black-hair'd Nathicana;
The sloe-ey'd, red-lipp'd Nathicana;
The silver-voic'd, sweet Nathicana;
The pale-rob'd, belov'd Nathicana.
And ever was she my belovèd,
From ages when Time was unfashion'd;

From days when the stars were not fashion'd
Nor any thing fashion'd but Yabon.
And here dwelt we ever and ever,
The innocent children of Zaïs,
At peace in the paths and the arbours,
White-crown'd with the blest nephalotë.
How oft would we float in the twilight
O'er flow'r-cover'd pastures and hillsides
All white with the lowly astalthon;
The lowly yet lovely astalthon,
And dream in a world made of dreaming
The dreams that are fairer than Aidenn;
Bright dreams that are truer than reason!
So dream'd and so lov'd we thro' ages,
Till came the curs'd season of Dzannin;
The daemon-damn'd season of Dzannin;
When red shone the suns and the planets,
And red gleamed the crescent Banapis,
And red fell the vapours of Yabon.
Then redden'd the blossoms and streamlets
And lakes that lay under the bridges,
And even the calm alabaster
Glow'd pink with uncanny reflections
Till all the carv'd fairies and daemons
Leer'd redly from the backgrounds of shadow.
Now redden'd my vision, and madly
I strove to peer thro' the dense curtain
And glimpse the divine Nathicana;
The pure, ever-pale Nathicana;
The lov'd, the unchang'd Nathicana.
But vortex on vortex of madness
Beclouded my labouring vision;
My damnable, reddening vision
That built a new world for my seeing;
A new world of redness and darkness,
A horrible coma call'd living.
So now in this coma call'd living
I view the bright phantoms of beauty;
The false, hollow phantoms of beauty
That cloak all the evils of Dzannin.
I view them with infinite longing,
So like do they seem to my lov'd one;
So shapely and fair like my lov'd one;
Yet foul from their eyes shines their evil;
Their cruel and pitiless evil,

More evil than Thaphron and Latgoz,
Twice ill for its gorgeous concealment.
And only in slumbers of midnight
Appears the lost maid Nathicana,
The pallid, the pure Nathicana,
Who fades at the glance of the dreamer.
Again and again do I seek her;
I woo with deep draughts of Plathotis,
Deep draughts brew'd in wine of Astarte
And strengthen'd with tears of long weeping.
I yearn for the gardens of Zaïs;
The lovely lost garden of Zaïs
Where blossoms the white nephalotë,
The redolent herald of midnight.
The last potent draught I am brewing;
A draught that the daemons delight in;
A draught that will banish the redness;
The horrible coma call'd living.
Soon, soon, if I fail not in brewing,
The redness and madness will vanish,
And deep in the worm-peopled darkness
Will rot the base chains that hav bound me.
Once more shall the gardens of Zaïs
Dawn white on my long-tortur'd vision,
And there midst the vapours of Yabon
Will stand the divine Nathicana;
The deathless, restor'd Nathicana
Whose like is not met with in living.

Observations

H.P. Lovecraft's poem "Nathicana" takes readers on a haunting and dreamlike journey into a fantastical realm turned cursed by cosmic horror, showcasing Lovecraft's mastery of surreal imagery. Despite being written around 1920, it was first published in 1927 in the *Vagrant* under the pseudonym "Albert Frederick Willie," a concoction by Lovecraft and Alfred Galpin, aimed at parodying "stylistic excesses" lacking "basic meaning." Lovecraft, in communications to Donald Wandrei, revealed the poem as a collaboration and attributed the pseudonym to a blend of Alfred's mother's maiden name and his first name. While the poem's repetitious melodic cadence suggests a target in Edgar Allan Poe, its craftsmanship rises to a high standard, transforming the satire into a masterful piece that Wandrei praises as "... rare and curious kind of literary freak, a satire too good, so that, instead of parodying, it possesses, the original."

"Nathicana" is set in the ethereal alabaster garden of Zaïs, where the narrator has an encounter with Nathicana, a divine figure of his dreamlike state who has won his affection and desire. However, the dreamscape shifts from love to horror with the cursed "season of Dzannin." The once peaceful realm turns nightmarish, transforming from alabaster to malevolent red. Madness, chaos, and horror envelop the idyllic scene, pulling Nathicana away. Trapped now in a "horrible coma call'd living," the narrator, distressed over his loss and encroaching madness, contemplates self-harm. Desperation leads him to brew a potent draught, seeking escape from reality to live eternally in the dream world with the deathless Nathicana.

Despite its creation in parody, "Nathicana" weaves a poignant tapestry of emotion. Through the exploration of love, desire, and loss, it resonates with those grappling with the complexities of relationships and the unpredictable nature of life. The narrator's descent into a "horrible coma call'd living" leading to contemplation of self-harm is a poignant reflection of the mental health struggles experienced by so many. His yearning for escape and immortality relates to the pursuit of permanence in the face of change. The dark themes of the poem, including madness and chaos, provide a metaphorical lens through which readers can confront their own experiences of the unsettling aspects of life. In its artistic expression, "Nathicana" transcends time, offering an evocative mirror for the human condition.

About Samantha Underhill

Samantha Underhill is an accomplished voice artist, poet, editor, professor, and author, spanning genres such as supernatural, cosmic horror, and drama. She is the literary editor for the dark aesthetic *Nyx Style* magazine, curating content with unique and mysterious themes. Her writings have found homes in her own poetry collections, as well as prestigious journals, including *Weird Tales Magazine* and various poetry and short story anthologies. As a professional voice artist, Samantha has narrated the works of notable authors, including Chris McAuley and Claudia Christian.

"Nyarlathotep"
by H.P. Lovecraft
Submitted and with Commentary
by Isaac Marion

A Prose Poem

Nyarlathotep ... the crawling chaos ... I am the last ... I will tell the audient void....

    I do not recall distinctly when it began, but it was months ago. The general tension was horrible. To a season of political and social upheaval was added a strange and brooding apprehension of hideous physical danger; a danger widespread and all-embracing, such a danger as may be imagined only in the most terrible phantasms of the night. I recall that the people went about with pale and worried faces, and whispered warnings and prophecies which no one dared consciously repeat or acknowledge to himself that he had heard. A sense of monstrous guilt was upon the land, and out of the abysses between the stars swept chill currents that made men shiver in dark and lonely places. There was a daemoniac alteration in the sequence of the seasons—the autumn heat lingered fearsomely, and everyone felt that the world and perhaps the universe had passed from the control of known gods or forces to that of gods or forces which were unknown.

    And it was then that Nyarlathotep came out of Egypt. Who he was, none could tell, but he was of the old native blood and looked like a Pharaoh. The fellahin knelt when they saw him, yet could not say why. He said he had risen up out of the blackness of twenty-seven centuries, and that he had heard messages from places not on this planet. Into the lands of civilisation came Nyarlathotep, swarthy, slender, and sinister, always buying strange instruments of glass and metal and combining them into instruments yet stranger. He spoke much of the sciences—of electricity and psychology—and gave exhibitions of power which sent his spectators away speechless, yet which swelled his fame to exceeding magnitude. Men advised one another to see Nyarlathotep, and shuddered. And where Nyarlathotep went, rest vanished; for the small hours were rent with the screams of nightmare. Never before had the screams of nightmare been such a public problem; now the wise men almost wished they could forbid sleep in the small hours, that the shrieks of cities might less horribly disturb the pale, pitying moon as it glimmered on green waters gliding under bridges, and old steeples crumbling against a sickly sky.

I remember when Nyarlathotep came to my city—the great, the old, the terrible city of unnumbered crimes. My friend had told me of him, and of the impelling fascination and allurement of his revelations, and I burned with eagerness to explore his uttermost mysteries. My friend said they were horrible and impressive beyond my most fevered imaginings; that what was thrown on a screen in the darkened room prophesied things none but Nyarlathotep dared prophesy, and that in the sputter of his sparks there was taken from men that which had never been taken before yet which shewed only in the eyes. And I heard it hinted abroad that those who knew Nyarlathotep looked on sights which others saw not.

It was in the hot autumn that I went through the night with the restless crowds to see Nyarlathotep; through the stifling night and up the endless stairs into the choking room. And shadowed on a screen, I saw hooded forms amidst ruins, and yellow evil faces peering from behind fallen monuments. And I saw the world battling against blackness; against the waves of destruction from ultimate space; whirling, churning; struggling around the dimming, cooling sun. Then the sparks played amazingly around the heads of the spectators, and hair stood up on end whilst shadows more grotesque than I can tell came out and squatted on the heads. And when I, who was colder and more scientific than the rest, mumbled a trembling protest about "imposture" and "static electricity," Nyarlathotep drave us all out, down the dizzy stairs into the damp, hot, deserted midnight streets. I screamed aloud that I was *not* afraid; that I never could be afraid; and others screamed with me for solace. We sware to one another that the city *was* exactly the same, and still alive; and when the electric lights began to fade we cursed the company over and over again, and laughed at the queer faces we made.

I believe we felt something coming down from the greenish moon, for when we began to depend on its light we drifted into curious involuntary formations and seemed to know our destinations though we dared not think of them. Once we looked at the pavement and found the blocks loose and displaced by grass, with scarce a line of rusted metal to shew where the tramways had run. And again we saw a tram-car, lone, windowless, dilapidated, and almost on its side. When we gazed around the horizon, we could not find the third tower by the river, and noticed that the silhouette of the second tower was ragged at the top. Then we split up into narrow columns, each of which seemed drawn in a different direction. One disappeared in a narrow alley to the left, leaving only the echo of a shocking moan. Another filed down a weed-choked subway entrance, howling with a laughter that was mad. My own column was sucked toward the open country, and presently felt a chill which was not of the hot autumn; for as we stalked out on the dark moor, we beheld around us the hellish moon-glitter of evil snows. Trackless, inexplicable snows, swept asunder in one direction only, where lay a gulf all the blacker for its glittering walls. The column seemed very thin indeed as it plodded dreamily into the gulf. I lingered behind, for the black rift in the green-litten snow was frightful, and I thought I had heard the reverberations of a disquieting wail as my companions vanished; but my power to linger was slight. As if beckoned by those who had gone before, I half floated between the titanic snowdrifts, quivering and afraid, into the sightless vortex of the unimaginable.

Screamingly sentient, dumbly delirious, only the gods that were can tell. A sickened, sensitive shadow writhing in hands that are not hands, and whirled blindly past ghastly midnights of rotting creation, corpses of dead worlds with sores that were cities, charnel winds that brush the pallid stars and make them flicker low. Beyond the worlds vague ghosts of monstrous things; half-seen columns of unsanctified temples that rest on nameless rocks beneath space and reach up to dizzy vacua above the spheres of light and darkness. And through this revolting graveyard of the universe the muffled, maddening beating of drums, and thin, monotonous whine of blasphemous flutes from inconceivable, unlighted chambers beyond Time; the detestable pounding and piping whereunto dance slowly, awkwardly, and absurdly the gigantic, tenebrous ultimate gods—the blind, voiceless, mindless gargoyles whose soul is Nyarlathotep.

Observations

The "prose poem" is a strange creature. It has the solid flesh of narrative, but with arcane runes of lyrical abstraction burned into it. You can see its shape, it moves around and does things, but if you try to capture it, your ropes may pass right through. It keeps one foot outside of this world.

Lovecraft has a vault of traditional verse poetry, and most of it left little impression on me. But "Nyarlathotep" stood out. There's a strikingly modern mood in his descriptions of a world in decline, a slow unraveling that feels like witnessing the heat death of the universe. The prose is less florid than usual—not a single exclamation point to be found. Instead of melodramatic wailing, it reads like a grim murmur.

The poem was inspired by a dream—Lovecraft supposedly wrote the beginning while still half asleep—and that stream-of-consciousness surrealism adds to the unease. It's a mode he employs only a few times in all his fiction, and it produces many of my favorite moments, slipping beneath the surface of writerly artifice, as if he's briefly tapping into some deeper, truer horror.

About Isaac Marion

Isaac Marion is the author of *The New York Times* bestselling Warm Bodies series, which inspired a major film and was translated into twenty-five languages. He lives mostly off-grid in central Washington, where he continues to write fiction while sharing stories on YouTube about living alone in the wilderness.

"On Being Brought from Africa to America" by Phillis Wheatley

Selected and with Commentary by Tananarive Due

'Twas mercy brought me from my *Pagan* land,
Taught my benighted soul to understand
That there's a God, that there's a *Saviour* too:
Once I redemption neither sought nor knew.
Some view our sable race with scornful eye,
"Their colour is a diabolic die."
Remember, *Christians*, *Negros*, black as *Cain*,
May be refin'd, and join th' angelic train.

Observations

Phillis Wheatley has always haunted me: she only lived to be thirty-one, but she was the first African American to publish a book of poetry in 1773 and was so celebrated that the Founding Fathers knew her name and work. Considering that Washington and Jefferson were both slaveholders, it's no surprise that Jefferson once said her poetry was "jeopardizing his assumption about African Americans." But not enough, apparently!

The ability to write poetry is not the measure of one's humanity; yet, since I first learned about Phillis Wheatley as a child, I was stupefied and enraged that her emergence did not rattle slavery to its roots. Black people were treated like chattel—and these Founders never stopped believing in our inferiority, clearly—but how could they justify such barbarity when confronted with this poet's gentle words?

It's no wonder that Wheatley had to appear before a court in Boston to prove that she actually had written her poems—an early version of the gaslighting Black artists often are still subjected to today. Lastly, this poem itself haunts me with its reference to the "mercy" of being brought from a "Pagan land" and aspirations of refinement to join "th' angelic train." Angelic? Hardly! But despite these notions, the power of these words from an enslaved woman who laid bare the lie of white supremacy—but who would not live to see the end of slavery even on the horizon—is a haunting far more devastating than any ghost.

About Tananarive Due

Tananarive Due is an American Book Award-winning author who teaches Black Horror and Afrofuturism at UCLA. Her most recent novel, *The Reformatory*, was a *New York Times* Notable Book.

"On Viewing the Skull and Bones of a Wolf" by Alexander Posey

Selected and with Commentary by Marsheila Rockwell

How savage, fierce and grim!
His bones are bleached and white.
But what is death to him?
He grins as if to bite.
He mocks the fate
That bade, "Begone."
There's fierceness stamped
In ev'ry bone.

Let silence settle from the midnight sky—
Such silence as you've broken with your cry;
The bleak wind howl, unto the ut'most verge
Of this mighty waste, thy fitting dirge.

Observations

Alexander Posey was a Muscogee Creek poet, journalist, and satirist; his mother was said to have hailed from the same family as US Poet Laureate Joy Harjo, born eighty years after Posey.

Despite the poem's imagery of death and solitude, it's doubtful Posey would have considered it horrific. He penned this poem during a time when his people's governments were being dissolved and their lands broken up in preparation for statehood—horrors of cultural erasure and forced assimilation that Posey regarded as far more traumatic than mere death, which for many Native people is simply a transition, not an end to be feared.

In this poem, though, we can imagine the Muscogee Creek—and all of Indian Country—as that wolf, mocking the colonizer that only thought the "savage" had been put down. What seems like nothing but skull and bones houses a spirit still full of fierceness, grinning as if to bite, its cry one that echoes across the mighty waste and promises that this isn't over yet. Not by a long shot.

About Marsheila Rockwell

Marsheila (Marcy) Rockwell (Chippewa/Red River Métis) is a Rhysling Award-winning poet and Scribe Award-nominated author. Her work includes novels set in the Marvel Universe and in the world of Dungeons & Dragons Online, as well as numerous short stories, poems, and comic book scripts. She lives in the desert with her family, buried under books.

"The Absence of Light"
by Millicent San Juan, PsyD
An Essay on Darkness

Darkness is the absence of light. It masks the dangers lurking nearby and obscures all possibility of shelter. In darkness, our primal instincts take over. It causes an override in our brain, a reversion to primal survival. We submit to a nexus of the three basic survival instincts: Fight your enemy, flee from the threat, or freeze so that the predator might overlook you. However, not all darkness is literal. Darkness can be a moment in time, or the gradual fading of the already dim light, or a reminder of a light that once was.

Darkness can descend suddenly, a sudden eclipse plunging us into a chasm of pain and torment. Psychologists call this chasm a *trauma*. Though we may climb from that chasm, the memory of it dwells within us. The memory corrodes us slowly, becoming a darkness itself. And though we may be far away in space and time from the chasm, the memory has become a being in itself. This entity slowly corrupts the sanctuary of our dreams into a cradle of nightmares. This type of darkness affects people in different ways, enraging some and paralyzing others. When this occurs, the trauma has become *posttraumatic stress disorder*. The memory of the chasm has fissured a chasm within our minds.

Not all darkness is sudden. Darkness can grow subtly, proliferating in an insidious manner until it is a writhing carpet of oozing mold that smothers the light within us. We try to escape its tendrils, but our limbs weigh heavy as it wraps around our bodies. It drags us down, and we are helpless as it slowly consumes the brightness of our spirit. We may stay awake, haunted by the lies that the darkness whispers to us. Or we might find comfort in sleep, finding the surrender of our consciousness to be the only reprieve from the darkness's frightening bellows. We may even question if the light within us is worth keeping aflame. Psychologists call moments like this a *major depressive episode*, with multiple episodes culminating in *major depressive disorder*. The darkness has wrapped itself around us, and we begin to lose sight of where it ends and where we begin.

Darkness may also fall when the light of someone else has been extinguished. Memories dance in our minds like shadows on a wall, only for us to realize that the shadows are merely an echo of the light that used to be there. Where there was warmth, there is only cold. Where there was safety, there is only anguish. Psychologists call this mourning *grief*, a natural reaction to a loved one's death.

There are many forms of darkness beyond what I have discussed. Some more severe, some less so. Darkness is an unavoidable element of existence, a phenomenon we all experience at some point in our lives. The poems in this anthology harness this darkness, using it as a vessel of exploration into the very essence of our human condition. These poems acknowledge the duality that yes, darkness is the absence of light ...

... but without darkness, light cannot exist.

About Millicent San Juan

Millicent "Billy" San Juan, PsyD, is an author and educator based out of San Diego, CA. He has served as a creative text writer and consultant for several Magic: the Gathering sets including *Lord of the Rings: Tales of Middle-earth*. He is a regular contributor to the *Pop Culture Psychology* book series, which analyzes popular culture through a psychological lens. He is a former president of the Horror Writers' Association's San Diego chapter and has paneled at various major conventions including San Diego Comic Con, WonderCon, and Fan Expo. He currently serves as the Patient Experience Manager for a local major hospital.

"One Need Not be a Chamber —to be Haunted"
by Emily Dickinson

Selected and with Commentary by Jess Landry

One need not be a chamber—to be haunted—
One need not be a House—
The Brain—has Corridors surpassing
Material Place—

Far safer, of a Midnight—meeting
External Ghost—
Than an Interior—confronting—
That cooler—Host—

Far safer, through an Abbey—gallop—
The Stones a'chase—
Than moonless—One's A'self encounter—
In lonesome place—

Ourself—behind Ourself—Concealed—
Should startle—most—
Assassin—hid in Our Apartment—
Be Horror's least—

The Prudent—carries a Revolver—
He bolts the Door,
O'erlooking a Superior Spectre
More near—

Observations

A ghost can be something more than the spirit stalking the halls or an apparition traipsing through a graveyard. Sometimes, as Emily Dickinson notes in this poem, the ghosts are much closer to home than we realize.

Mental health care has not been humanity's strong suit, and even less so when Dickinson wrote this poem in 1862. Yet the imagery and themes she presents here—of the loneliness that's hidden within the lines; of the brain having many corridors, many rooms, many complexities; of an intruder breaking in, a sight unseen with malicious intent, much like an illness that we can't see; of that intruder drawing nearer and nearer, and us, being helpless against it—all still ring true to this day.

Though on the shorter side, "One Need Not be a Chamber—to be Haunted" will forever be poignant. Dickinson's mastery of words wraps a subtle warning within the vast confines of a haunted house—real ghosts are not so much to fear, but the ghosts that live in our heads are the ones we need to look out for.

About Jess Landry

Jess Landry is a screenwriter, director, Bram Stoker Award-winning author, and Shirley Jackson Award-nominated editor. Her latest collection of short stories, *The Night Belongs To Us*, is out now from Crystal Lake Publishing, and her slasher film, *Body Count*, is set to stream on Tubi in 2024.

"Ozymandias"
by Percy Bysshe Shelley
Selected and with Commentary by Bev Vincent

I met a traveller from an antique land,
Who said—"Two vast and trunkless legs of stone
Stand in the desert.... Near them, on the sand,
Half sunk a shattered visage lies, whose frown,
And wrinkled lip, and sneer of cold command,
Tell that its sculptor well those passions read
Which yet survive, stamped on these lifeless things,
The hand that mocked them, and the heart that fed;
And on the pedestal, these words appear:
My name is Ozymandias, King of Kings;
Look on my Works, ye Mighty, and despair!
Nothing beside remains. Round the decay
Of that colossal Wreck, boundless and bare
The lone and level sands stretch far away.

Observations

My high school English courses focused mostly on poetry. I remember spending full classes analyzing and parsing the meaning of poems ... sometimes an hour on only a few lines. I was—and continue to be—astonished by how much symbolism and meaning could be packed into certain poems. I don't consider myself an expert on those poems, which have been analyzed by many people far more qualified than I over the centuries, but I have a visceral memory of those long-ago classes (has it really been over forty-five years ago?). The impact of certain poems on me cannot be overstated. When "Ozymandias" popped up as the title of an episode of the TV series *Breaking Bad*, my poetic antennae went up! I knew where this was going.

My tenth-grade English teacher, Mr. Comeau, a man who paced back and forth in front of the classroom with his head bobbing like a pigeon, described Shelley as a romantic poet whose writing was often overblown, flowery, and effete. But there's nothing overblown about "Ozymandias." It's stripped to the bone, unromantic and devastating—a damning portrayal of hubris and the futility of power. Is it horror? I'd argue that, yes, it's nigh-unto post-apocalyptic, with its closing depiction of "lone and level sands" and the sneering, shattered visage captured in this lifeless effigy. I can —and often do—picture it in my mind. It has given me nightmares.

About Bev Vincent

Bev Vincent is the author of several books, including *The Road to the Dark Tower* and *Stephen King: A Complete Exploration of His Work, Life, and Influences*. He coedited the anthology *Flight or Fright with King* and has published over 130 stories, with appearances in magazines such as *Cemetery Dance*, *Ellery Queen's*, and *Alfred Hitchcock's* and *Black Cat Mystery Magazines*. He has been published in twenty languages and nominated for the Stoker (twice), Edgar, Ignotus, Locus, Rondo Hatton, and ITW Thriller Awards. Learn more at bevvincent.com.

"Poor Jack" by H.C. Dodge
Selected and with Commentary by Grady Hendrix

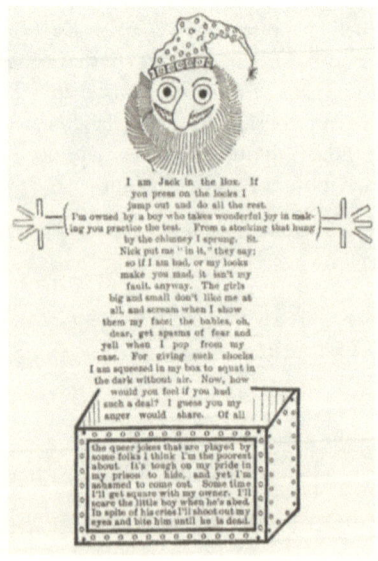

Observations

No one much remembers Herwick C. Dodge, and why should they? Born in New York City, he worked for a textile manufacturer, but in the 1880s and 1890s he turned out around three hundred poems for newspapers and magazines ranging from *Puck* to *Canadian Crescent*. He was most famous for his "figure poems" published in the shape of a woman wearing a corset, a beehive, a baseball diamond, or a corpse hanging from a gibbet. It was a gimmick, but a wildly popular one, which an editor at *Punch* noted caused "the compositor to indulge in thoughts of murder."

Dodge's figure poems were either humorous (fishermen drinking so much they ignore their catch) or moral (the evil of corsets) but "Poor Jack" is a psychotic little example of a "Christmas number," one of the horror stories that jammed nearly every Victorian newspaper from December to January. Dickens had already written about his childhood terror of toys in his 1850 essay "The Christmas Tree," but Dodge's poem sends that fear of toys into hyperdrive. Forced to follow the shape of a jack-in-the-box, its sentences break in strange places, giving it a weird, slightly lunatic rhythm that becomes more menacing as it builds toward an outburst of rage in the final lines. Reading it is like listening to someone reciting "A Visit From Saint Nicholas" and only halfway through, realizing that you're listening to an escaped madman who's holding an axe behind his back, and your life will end when the poem does.

About Grady Hendrix

Grady Hendrix is *The New York Times* bestselling author of *How To Sell a Haunted House*, *The Final Girl Support Group*, *The Southern Book Club's Guide to Slaying Vampires*, and a whole host of other horror novels. His history of the horror paperback boom of the '70s and '80s, *Paperbacks from Hell*, won the Stoker Award for Outstanding Achievement in Nonfiction (and he really wishes his publisher would let him write a sequel). He is also the screenwriter of *Mohawk* (2017) and *Satanic Panic* (2019). You can learn more about him at gradyhendrix.com.

"Porphyria's Lover"
by Robert Browning
Selected and with Commentary
by Brenna Yovanoff

The rain set early in to-night,
The sullen wind was soon awake,
It tore the elm-tops down for spite,
And did its worst to vex the lake:
I listened with heart fit to break.
When glided in Porphyria; straight
She shut the cold out and the storm,
And kneeled and made the cheerless grate
Blaze up, and all the cottage warm;
Which done, she rose, and from her form
Withdrew the dripping cloak and shawl,
And laid her soiled gloves by, untied
Her hat and let the damp hair fall,
And, last, she sat down by my side
And called me. When no voice replied,
She put my arm about her waist,
And made her smooth white shoulder bare,
And all her yellow hair displaced,
And, stooping, made my cheek lie there,
And spread, o'er all, her yellow hair,
Murmuring how she loved me—she
Too weak, for all her heart's endeavour,
To set its struggling passion free
From pride, and vainer ties dissever,
And give herself to me for ever.
But passion sometimes would prevail,
Nor could to-night's gay feast restrain
A sudden thought of one so pale

For love of her, and all in vain:
So, she was come through wind and rain.
Be sure I looked up at her eyes
Happy and proud; at last I knew
Porphyria worshipped me; surprise
Made my heart swell, and still it grew
While I debated what to do.
That moment she was mine, mine, fair,
Perfectly pure and good: I found
A thing to do, and all her hair
In one long yellow string I wound
Three times her little throat around,
And strangled her. No pain felt she;
I am quite sure she felt no pain.
As a shut bud that holds a bee,
I warily oped her lids: again
Laughed the blue eyes without a stain.
And I untightened next the tress
About her neck; her cheek once more
Blushed bright beneath my burning kiss:
I propped her head up as before,
Only, this time my shoulder bore
Her head, which droops upon it still:
The smiling rosy little head,
So glad it has its utmost will,
That all it scorned at once is fled,
And I, its love, am gained instead!
Porphyria's love: she guessed not how
Her darling one wish would be heard.
And thus we sit together now,
And all night long we have not stirred,
And yet God has not said a word!

Observations

When I was seventeen, I had very long, very yellow hair. This is not literary analysis, it's just the truth. That year, we were assigned "Porphyria's Lover" in my English class, and on the facing page was a reproduction of John Everitt Millais's painting "The Bridesmaid," which depicts a girl with very long, very yellow hair. (Maybe you see where this is going ... I, however, did not.)

Any resemblance between the painting and myself was really more "close call" than absolute likeness, but our teacher was delighted and proposed a reenactment. I'd never been very theatrical, but I also wasn't particularly self-conscious. I was curious. I liked to see *where a thing was going*. Which is how I wound up in front of a roomful of thirty people, getting fake-strangled with my own hair by the guy who sat behind me, while the girls on the tennis team took turns reading aloud.

I've never forgotten this weird tableau, which means I've never forgotten Robert Browning or his impressive setlist of murder poems. My English class called me Porphyria until graduation, but in the interest of literary accuracy, I should point out that my hair only went around two and a half times.

About Brenna Yovanoff

Brenna Yovanoff was raised in a barn. She spent her formative years in Arkansas, in a town heavily populated by snakes, where sometimes they would drop turkeys out of the sky. When she was five, she moved to Colorado, where it snows on a regular basis but never snows turkeys. She is *The New York Times* bestselling author of six novels, including *The Replacement*, *Places No One Knows*, and her most recent book, *Stranger Things: Runaway Max*. She lives in Denver with her family.

"Resumé" by Dorothy Parker
Selected and with Commentary by John Skipp

Razors pain you;
Rivers are damp;
Acids stain you;
And drugs cause cramp.
Guns aren't lawful;
Nooses give;
Gas smells awful;
You might as well live.

Observations

Not all horror is scary in the conventional sense. From the whimsically macabre cartoons of Charles Addams, Gahan Wilson, and Gary Larson to the gore-soaked "splatstick" of early Stuart Gordon and Peter Jackson films, gruesome good cheer has always been a welcome and necessary evil in the shadow realm.

As the sharpest, driest wit and deepest, darkest cocktail of sorrow ever to hold court at the Algonquin Round Table, way back in the roaring 1920s, Dorothy Parker would doubtless roll her eyes at such comparisons, had she only a time machine and the slightest desire to use it.

But her genius was for sly and ruthlessly rueful observation. And here—in itemizing her personal litany of suicide methods either tried or contemplated—she expertly squeezes her razored rhyming and coal-black longing for merciful death into one perfect shining diamond that makes me bark with knowing laughter every single time I read it. When it comes to dark poets, she is my undisputed queen.

About John Skipp

John Skipp is a Saturn Award winning filmmaker (*Tales of Halloween*), Stoker Award winning anthologist (*Demons, Mondo Zombie*), and *The New York Times* bestselling author (*The Light at the End, The Scream*) whose books have sold millions of copies in a dozen languages worldwide. His first anthology, *Book of the Dead*, laid the foundation in 1989 for modern zombie literature. He's also editor-in-chief of Fungasm Press. From splatterpunk founding father to bizarro elder statesman, Skipp has influenced a generation of horror and counterculture artists around the world. His latest book is *Don't Push the Button*. His latest movie is *The Great Divide*.

"RICHARD CORY"
BY EDWIN ARLINGTON ROBINSON
Selected and with Commentary by Hallie Ephron

Whenever Richard Cory went down town,
We people on the pavement looked at him:
He was a gentleman from sole to crown,
Clean favored, and imperially slim.
And he was always quietly arrayed,
And he was always human when he talked;
But still he fluttered pulses when he said,
"Good-morning," and he glittered when he walked.
And he was rich—yes, richer than a king—
And admirably schooled in every grace:
In fine, we thought that he was everything
To make us wish that we were in his place.
So on we worked, and waited for the light,
And went without the meat, and cursed the bread;
And Richard Cory, one calm summer night,
Went home and put a bullet through his head.

OBSERVATIONS

My mother was a screenwriter who'd majored in English at Hunter (NYC). She loved the spoken word. One of my fondest memories is of her reciting poems after dinner at the table.

A favorite poet was the dyspeptic Edward Arlington Robinson who wrote with a jaundiced eye about the toffs and ne'er-do-wells he disdained. His works tend to circle around and end with a zinger, not unlike the mystery novels I write.

Here's "Richard Cory," one I know by heart and have recited it so many times to my children that they know it, too.

About Hallie Ephron

Hallie Ephron writes suspense novels she hopes keep readers up nights. A *New York Times* bestselling author, reviewers have called her books "deliciously creepy." Her newest, *Careful What You Wish For*, is a mash-up of *Antiques Roadshow* and *Strangers on a Train*.

Her *Never Tell a Lie* was adapted for film for the Lifetime Movie Network. She is a five-time finalist for the Mary Higgins Clark Award, and reviewed crime fiction for *The Boston Globe* for a dozen years.

"Rizpah"
by Alfred Lord Tennyson
Selected and with Commentary
by Ramsey Campbell

Wailing, wailing, wailing, the wind over land and sea—
And Willy's voice in the wind, "O mother, come out
    to me."
Why should he call me to-night, when he knows that I
    cannot go?
For the downs are as bright as day, and the full moon stares
    at the snow.
We should be seen, my dear; they would spy us out of the
    town.
The loud black nights for us, and the storm rushing over the
    down,
When I cannot see my own hand, but am led by the creak of
    the chain,
And grovel and grope for my son till I find myself drench'd
    with the rain.
Anything fallen again? nay—what was there left to fall?
I have taken them home, I have number'd the bones, I have
    hidden them all.
What am I saying? and what are you? do you come as a spy?
Falls? what falls? who knows? As the tree falls so must it lie.
Who let her in? how long has she been? you—what have
    you heard?
Why did you sit so quiet? you never have spoken a word.
O—to pray with me—yes—a lady—none of their spies—
But the night has crept into my heart, and begun to darken
    my eyes.
Ah—you, that have liv'd so soft, what should you know of
    the night,

The blast and the burning shame and the bitter frost and the fright?
I have done it, while you were asleep—you were only made for the day.
I have gather'd my baby together—and now you may go your way.
Nay—for it's kind of you, Madam, to sit by an old dying wife.
But say nothing hard of my boy, I have only an hour of life.
I kiss'd my boy in the prison, before he went out to die.
"They dar'd me to do it," he said, and he never has told me a lie.
I whipp'd him for robbing an orchard once when he was but a child—
"The farmer dar'd me to do it," he said; he was always so wild—
And idle—and couldn't be idle—my Willy—he never could rest.
The King should have made him a soldier; he would have been one of his best.
But he liv'd with a lot of wild mates, and they never would let him be good;
They swore that he dare not rob the mail, and he swore that he would;
And he took no life, but he took one purse, and when all was done
He flung it among his fellows—I'll none of it, said my son.
I came into court to the Judge and the lawyers. I told them my tale,
God's own truth—but they kill'd him, they kill'd him for robbing the mail.
They hang'd him in chains for a show—he had always borne a good name—
To be hang'd for a thief—and then put away—isn't that enough shame?
Dust to dust—low down—let us hide! but they set him so high
That all the ships of the world could stare at him, passing by.
God 'ill pardon the hell-black raven and horrible fowls of the air,
But not the black heart of the lawyer who kill'd him and hang'd him there.
And the jailer forced me away. I had bid him my last goodbye;

They had fasten'd the door of his cell, "O mother!" I heard him cry.
I couldn't get back tho' I tried, he had something further to say,
And now I never shall know it. The jailer forced me away.
Then since I couldn't but hear that cry of my boy that was dead,
They seiz'd me and shut me up: they fasten'd me down on my bed.
"Mother, O mother!"—he call'd in the dark to me year after year—
They beat me for that, they beat me—you know that I couldn't but hear;
And then at the last they found I had grown so stupid and still
They let me abroad again—but the creatures had work'd their will.
Flesh of my flesh was gone, but bone of my bone was left—
I stole them all from the lawyers—and you, will you call it a theft?—
My baby, the bones that had suck'd me, the bones that had laugh'd and had cried—
Theirs? O no! they are mine—not theirs—they had mov'd in my side.
Do you think I was scar'd by the bones? I kiss'd 'em, I buried 'em all—
I can't dig deep, I am old—in the night by the churchyard wall.
My Willy 'ill rise up whole when the trumpet of judgment 'ill sound,
But I charge you never to say that I laid him in holy ground.
They would scratch him up—they would hang him again on the cursed tree.
Sin? O yes—we are sinners, I know—let all that be,
And read me a Bible verse of the Lord's good will toward men—
"Full of compassion and mercy, the Lord"—let me hear it again;
"Full of compassion and mercy—long-suffering." Yes, O yes!
For the lawyer is born but to murder—the Saviour lives but to bless.
He'll never put on the black cap except for the worst of the worst,

And the first may be last—I have heard it in church—and
    the last may be first.
Suffering—O long-suffering—yes, as the Lord must know,
Year after year in the mist and the wind and the shower and
    the snow.
Heard, have you? what? they have told you he never
    repented his sin.
How do they know it? are they his mother? are you of
    his kin?
Heard! have you ever heard, when the storm on the downs
    began,
The wind that 'ill wail like a child and the sea that 'ill moan
    like a man?
Election, Election and Reprobation—it's all very well.
But I go to-night to my boy, and I shall not find him in Hell.
For I car'd so much for my boy that the Lord has look'd into
    my care,
And He means me, I'm sure, to be happy with Willy, I
    know not where.
And if he be lost—but to save my soul, that is all your
    desire:
Do you think that I care for my soul if my boy be gone to
    the fire?
I have been with God in the dark—go, go, you may leave me
    alone—
You never have borne a child—you are just as hard as a
    stone.
Madam, I beg your pardon! I think that you mean to be
    kind,
But I cannot hear what you say for my Willy's voice in the
    wind—
The snow and the sky so bright—he us'd but to call in the
    dark,
And he calls to me now from the church and not from the
    gibbet—for hark!
Nay—you can hear it yourself—it is coming—shaking the
    walls—
Willy—the moon's in a cloud—Good-night. I am going.
    He calls.

Observations

"... a poet who (in our own humble and sincere opinion) is *the greatest* that ever lived." So, Edgar Allan Poe wrote of Tennyson in 1845, but he didn't live to read "Rizpah," which is surely reminiscent of his own tales told by the deranged ("The Tell-Tale Heart," for instance). May we find his influence in Tennyson's paranoid monologue? I'd argue that just as Poe refined the Gothic tale, pretty well creating the modern short story in the process, Tennyson rendered Poe's style of narration more naturalistic while containing it within a strict poetic scheme. Part of the power of "Rizpah" derives from the tension between conversational speech and heightened language, a drift expressive of the dying mother's errant mental state. I first read the poem in *Dark of the Moon*, August Derleth's seminal anthology of macabre and uncanny verse, and it has haunted me ever since with its poignancy and eeriness and authentic chills bordering on the spectral. I've often wished I could introduce it to a wider audience, and that's just one reason I welcome the present book.

About Ramsey Campbell

The Oxford Companion to English Literature describes Ramsey Campbell as "Britain's most respected living horror writer," and *The Washington Post* sums up his work as "one of the monumental accomplishments of modern popular fiction." His awards include the Grand Master Award of the World Horror Convention, the Lifetime Achievement Award of the Horror Writers Association, the Living Legend Award of the International Horror Guild, and the World Fantasy Lifetime Achievement Award. In 2015 he was made an Honorary Fellow of Liverpool John Moores University for outstanding services to literature. Among his novels are *The Face That Must Die, Incarnate, Midnight Sun, The Count of Eleven, The Darkest Part of the Woods, The Overnight, Secret Story, The Grin of the Dark, Thieving Fear, Creatures of the Pool, The Seven Days of Cain, Ghosts Know, The Kind Folk, Think Yourself Lucky, Thirteen Days by Sunset Beach, The Wise Friend, Somebody's Voice, Fellstones,* and *The Lonely Lands*. His Brichester Mythos trilogy consists of *The Searching Dead, Born to the Dark,* and *The Way of the Worm*. His collections include *Waking Nightmares, Ghosts and Grisly Things, Told by the Dead, Just Behind You, Holes for Faces, By the Light of My Skull, Fearful Implications,* and a two-volume retrospective roundup (*Phantasmagorical Stories*), as well as *The Village Killings and Other Novellas*. His nonfiction is collected as *Ramsey Campbell, Probably* and *Ramsey Campbell, Certainly*, while *Ramsey's Rambles* collects his video reviews, and *Six Stooges and Counting* is a book-length study of the Three

Stooges. *Limericks of the Alarming and Phantasmal* is a history of horror fiction in the form of fifty limericks.

"Sick Room"
by Langston Hughes
Selected and with Commentary
by Linda D. Addison

How quiet
It is in this sick room
Where on the bed
A silent woman lies between two lovers—
Life and Death,
And all three covered with a sheet of pain.

Observations

While Langston Hughes is known for his powerful writings of Black life in America from the 1920s through the 1960s, I have found inspiration from his haiku and poems for my own horror/weird writing in the past.

This short poem in particular, beautifully invokes the agonizing emotions of being in pain and lingering between Life and Death. I love the surreal depiction of the two as lovers, both desiring the woman. The last line is the way I like to end my own poetry, with an image that cannot be, yet is perfect.

About Linda D. Addison

Linda D. Addison is the author of five award-winning collections, including *The Place of Broken Things* written with Alessandro Manzetti, recipient of the HWA Lifetime Achievement Award and SFPA Grand Master of Fantastic Poetry. Her site: LindaAddisonWriter.com.

"Spellbound" by Emily Brontë
Submitted and with Commentary by Christina Sng

The night is darkening round me,
The wild winds coldly blow;
But a tyrant spell has bound me
And I cannot, cannot go.
The giant trees are bending
Their bare boughs weighed with snow.
And the storm is fast descending,
And yet I cannot go.
Clouds beyond clouds above me,
Wastes beyond wastes below;
But nothing drear can move me;
I will not, cannot go.

Observations

Emily Brontë's "Spellbound" takes us to a scene of great destruction and keeps us there with her potent, powerful words.

I feel this poem so vividly. It reflects our response to trauma—why we stay in violent situations, run toward danger, flee when we should help. And our reaction to the climate crisis. Little is done as we stand amid floods, heatwaves, and storms.

"Spellbound" shows us how we freeze in the face of annihilation, even when it is upon us. How we sit in the maelstrom, unable to see how it destroys us.

About Christina Sng

Christina Sng is a three-time Bram Stoker Award-winning poet, writer, essayist, and artist. Her work appears in numerous venues worldwide, including *Interstellar Flight Magazine, Penumbric, Southwest Review, Weird Tales,* and *The Washington Post.*

"STAGOLEE"
BY AUTHOR UNKNOWN
SELECTED AND WITH COMMENTARY BY GARY PHILLIPS

Stagolee, Stagolee, what's dat in yo' grip?
Nothin' but my Sunday clothes, I'm goin' to take a trip,
O dat man, bad man, Stagolee done come.
Stagolee, Stagolee, where you been so long?
I been out on de battle fiel' shootin' an' havin' fun,
O dat man, bad man, Stagolee done come.
Stagolee was a bully man, an' ev'y body knowed,
When dey seed Stagolee comin', to give Stagolee de road,
O dat man, bad man, Stagolee done come.
Stagolee started out, he give his wife his han',
"Good-by, darlin', I'm goin' to kill a man."
Stagolee killed a man an' laid him on de flo',
What's dat he kill him wid? Dat same ole fohty-fo'.
Stagolee killed a man an' laid him on his side,
What's dat he kill him wid? Dat same ole fohty-five.
Out of house an' down de street Stagolee did run,
In his hand he held a great big smokin' gun.
Stagolee, Stagolee, I'll tell you what I'll do,
If you'll git me out'n dis trouble I'll do as much for you.
Ain't it a pity, ain't it a shame?
Stagolee was shot, but he don't want no name.
Stagolee, Stagolee, look what you done done,
Killed de best ole citerzen; now you'll hav' to be hung.
Stagolee cried to de jury an' to de judge: Please don't take my life,
I have only three little children an' one little lovin' wife,
O dat man, bad man, Stagolee done come.

Observations

The foregoing opening lines of a first-person version of a legend who's been lauded by the likes of Lloyd Price (a sanitized rendition) to Nick Cave (an X-rated take) and many more singers. Stack-O-Lee—or maybe it's Stager Lee—is the bad man who set the mold for cold-eyed motherlovers and pitiless anti-heroes to come.

The story about him is said to have originated from a real incident in 1895 involving a pimp named "Stack" Lee Shelton and his friend Billy Lyons as they had a drink in a bar in St. Louis. In some versions, Stack is a democrat and Billy a republican. In most versions, Stack is draped and wearing a white Stetson hat. An argument ensued, maybe it was over a woman or maybe it was over politics. And at some point, either Billy snatched the Stetson off Stack's head, or he won it gambling. Either way, Billy would soon be dead on the floor, done in by Stack's blue-steel forty-four.

Some accounts have the killer going to prison and some have him hanged and going to hell. While there he didn't blink and jumped in the sack with the Devil's wife. Stagolee's reputation would be cemented in ribald retellings in poems, rap, and even a graphic novel. Along the way Stagolee would be remixed via revisionist reinterpretations, symbolizing the man who wouldn't back down. The verve of Stagolee lives on in many a rough cat and kitty, no matter their color—in and out of fiction.

About Gary Phillips

Gary Phillips has written various novels, short stories, comics, and edited anthologies such as the award-winning *The Obama Inheritance: Fifteen Stories of Conspiracy Noir*. He was a staff writer on *Snowfall*, an FX show streaming on Hulu about crack and the CIA in 1980s South Central where he grew up. And *Culprits*, also streaming on Hulu, is based on source material he conceived and coedited, the linked anthology *Culprits: The Heist was Just the Beginning*. His latest novel, *Ash Dark as Night*, received a starred review in *Publishers Weekly*.

"Storm Fear" by Robert Frost
Selected with Commentary
by Jezzy Wolfe

When the wind works against us in the dark,
And pelts the snow
The lower chamber window on the east,
And whispers with a sort of stifled bark,
The beast,
'Come out! Come out!'—
It costs no inward struggle not to go,
Ah, no!
I count our strength,
Two and a child,
Those of us not asleep subdued to mark
How the cold creeps as the fire dies at length,—
How drifts are piled,
Dooryard and road ungraded,
Till even the comforting barn grows far away
And my heart owns a doubt
Whether 'tis in us to arise with day
And save ourselves unaided.

Observations

Frost is famously known for poignant, reflective poetry about solitude and the fleeting nature of our existence. His poems, "Stopping by Woods on a Snowy Evening," "Nothing Gold Can Stay," and "The Road Not Taken" have been referenced time and again in popular films such as *Dead Poets Society*, television show favorites such as *M.A.S.H.* and *Buffy the Vampire*

Slayer, and fine literary works such as *The Outsiders* and the Dresden Files. Though never a scholar, he was a four-time Pulitzer Prize winner and inarguably one of the greatest American poets of all time. But while he often inked his poetry with introspection and melancholy, he did, on occasion, tuck darker themes between the lines of his most beloved verses.

Which brings me to one of his earliest poems, "Storm Fear." Here we have, on the surface, a lyric chronicling a young father's stronghold against a ravaging winter storm in the middle of the night. "The beast" mentioned is the furious blizzard outside his home ... and that is a terrifying scenario, indeed. Us vs. Nature. We know the elements win if we give in to the curiosity of what lays beyond our door in the dark, yet still we struggle to remain resistant to its call.

You could argue, however, that the storm in question is not a winter's blizzard, but that very struggle with our attraction to danger. The voice in our head becomes the beast luring us toward the unknown, facing threats we cannot identify, and therefore cannot defeat. The familiar sight of the "comfortable barn" growing far away might then become a metaphor for the inability to yield to the voice of reason that strengthens our instincts. Our urge to pursue the dangers beyond the safety of our doors is often the greatest risk to our survival. And what is horror, if not the most primal fear that we won't survive whatever beast is out there calling us into the darkness?

About Jezzy Wolfe

Jezzy Wolfe is a poet and author whose works have appeared in various publications since 2009, such as *Space and Time Magazine*, *Weird Tales*, and numerous anthologies from publishers such as Smart Rhino and Crystal Lake Publishing. Her collections *Monstrum Poetica* and *Strange Doses* can be purchased through various online booksellers.

"Suicide's Note"
by Langston Hughes
Selected and with Commentary
by Amber Benson

The calm,
Cool face of the river
Asked me for a kiss.

Observations

I've been fascinated by this poem for decades. I can't remember how I originally came across it, but there was just something about the controlled terseness of the words that captured me. On the face of it, this poem seems very simple. The title encapsulates the subject matter completely. The content is straightforward and logical. Speak these beautifully crafted words out loud, multiple times, in a round, and it becomes a mantra.

But then there's that damn comma ... and somehow its placement changes everything for me. With the comma, the first line becomes a moment of decision crystalized into words: the calm of a psyche embracing its own demise. This isn't just an artful rumination on suicide, but a window into the mind of someone who's screwed their courage to the sticking place and is ready to complete the act. With this knowledge, we leave behind any notion these are just simple words. This is the suffering of a human soul elevated into art—and though it may be beautiful, there's nothing simple about it.

About Amber Benson

Amber Benson is a writer, director, actor, and maker of things. In her spare time, she writes true crime movies for Lifetime Television, reads detective fiction, and cooks weird food that may or may not be edible—depends on the day. In her previous life, she played Tara Maclay for three seasons on the TV show *Buffy the Vampire Slayer*.

"The City in the Sea"
by Edgar Allan Poe
Selected and with Commentary
by Kami Garcia

Lo! Death has reared himself a throne
In a strange city lying alone
Far down within the dim West,
Where the good and the bad and the worst and the best
Have gone to their eternal rest.
There shrines and palaces and towers
(Time-eaten towers and tremble not!)
Resemble nothing that is ours.
Around, by lifting winds forgot,
Resignedly beneath the sky
The melancholy waters lie.
No rays from the holy Heaven come down
On the long night-time of that town;
But light from out the lurid sea
Streams up the turrets silently—
Gleams up the pinnacles far and free—
Up domes—up spires—up kingly halls—
Up fanes—up Babylon-like walls—
Up shadowy long-forgotten bowers
Of sculptured ivy and stone flowers—
Up many and many a marvellous shrine
Whose wreathed friezes intertwine
The viol, the violet, and the vine.
Resignedly beneath the sky
The melancholy waters lie.
So blend the turrets and shadows there
That all seem pendulous in air,
While from a proud tower in the town

Death looks gigantically down.
There open fanes and gaping graves
Yawn level with the luminous waves;
But not the riches there that lie
In each idol's diamond eye—
Not the gaily-jewelled dead
Tempt the waters from their bed;
For no ripples curl, alas!
Along that wilderness of glass—
No swellings tell that winds may be
Upon some far-off happier sea—
No heavings hint that winds have been
On seas less hideously serene.
But lo, a stir is in the air!
The wave—there is a movement there!
As if the towers had thrust aside,
In slightly sinking, the dull tide—
As if their tops had feebly given
A void within the filmy Heaven.
The waves have now a redder glow—
The hours are breathing faint and low—
And when, amid no earthly moans,
Down, down that town shall settle hence,
Hell, rising from a thousand thrones,
Shall do it reverence.

Observations

Edgar Allan Poe's lyric poem "The City in the Sea" was published in 1845, during American Romanticism, a literary, art, and philosophical movement in the United States that took place between 1830 and 1870. American Romanticism focused on emotion over reason, individualism and self-exploration, the importance of nature, and the exploration of spirituality and the unknown. The period defined the voice of American literature for the first time and Edgar Allan Poe was one of its defining voices.

"The City in the Sea" is about a haunting, desolate, and unnatural city ruled by Death that is slowly sinking into a sea that represents a Hell-like place. The poem explores themes of sin, death, and the decay of the human soul, and it is considered one of Poe's greatest early works.

I grew up writing poetry, and my reading genres of choice were horror and southern Gothic, so it didn't take me long to discover Poe. His work fascinated me because I found writing lyric poetry challenging and so much of the lyric poetry I had read up to that point felt too rosy and optimistic for my teenage taste. Poe wrote lyric poetry that read like a Stephen King novel—the kind of writing that gave me nightmares. When I discovered "The City in the Sea," it did not disappoint, and when I reread it today, it still doesn't.

In the world we live in today, we see examples of cruelty and moral depravity on a daily basis and some part of me hopes there is a "city in the sea" where the people who hurt the innocent and defenseless will end up. An isolated, desolate place that will sink into Poe's sea like Sodom and Gomorrah. I love the fact that Mike Flanagan's popular Netflix limited series *The Fall of the House of Usher* sparked renewed interest in "The City in the Sea." The poem is prominently featured in the final episode and represents the fall of the Usher family after a lifetime of greed and immorality.

About Kami Garcia

Kami Garcia is a #1 *New York Times*, *USA Today*, and international bestselling author and comic book writer. As an award-winning, Bram Stoker Award-nominated young adult author of sixteen novels and graphic novels, she has been published in fifty-one countries and thirty-eight languages, and her books have sold more than ten million copies worldwide. Kami's best-known works include *Beautiful Creatures*, the first book of the Caster Chronicles series, her ongoing Teen Titans graphic novel series for DC, and *Joker/Harley: Criminal Sanity*. Follow her on Instagram & X @kamigarcia.

"Ghost Road" by Lisa Fredsti
Selected and with Commentary
by Dana Fredsti

Ghost road
In the middle of the night
Stretched out in the darkness like a body on the landscape
Ghost road ...
Ghost road
Smells like sage and salt
Up on the hillside the bulldozer's waiting
Ghost road ...
Am I alive?
Am I alive?
I'm told the living feel pain
I survive
I survive
Oh god.
I'm going take the road again
Ghost road
I am standing still
Outside my window the world keeps passing by
Ghost road ...
Ghost road
I don't wanna know
Gotta watch the road ahead I can't keep looking back
Am I alive?
Am I alive?
I'm told the living feel pain
I survive
I survive
Oh god.

I'm going take the road again
Ghost road
Goodbye forever
No one will remember the way you used to be
Ghost road ...
Ghost road ...

OBSERVATIONS

I didn't really understand or appreciate the beauty and functionality of metaphors when I was a kid. A literal-minded child, I wanted everything laid out clearly. No fancy language for me, no sir! But now and again I'd come across a poem that spoke to me—usually something kind of morbid—like Yeats' *The Second Coming* or *The Cremation of Sam McGee* by Robert W. Service. Then I joined The Pickups, a band started by my sister Lisa, with guitarist Tony Mandracchia and drummer Tod Tatum. Lisa wrote the words and the music, played bass, and was lead vocalist. I was the backup vocalist and percussionist.

Having no knack for writing poetry/lyrics—I wrote one song, which started like this: *"I want to be a zombie, gon' join da living dead. I want to be a zombie, don't shoot me in da head."*— I could only sit back and admire her songwriting ability. Her lyrics resonated in a way that most poetry did not, partly because her voice and the instrumental arrangement made the words (sorry) sing. I love all of her songs, but my favorite Ghost Road, which Lisa used to introduce at gigs as being a song about "depression and condominiums." We grew up in San Diego and saw much of the open land of our youth built up into malls and condos, so this made sense to me.

For me, however, the song is also about change, good and bad, and the need to let go of the past. The line that gets me every time, that actually makes me tear up whenever I listen to the CD, is this one:

Gotta watch the road ahead I can't keep looking back...

ABOUT DANA FREDSTI

I didn't really understand or appreciate the beauty and functionality of metaphors when I was a kid. A literal-minded child, I wanted everything laid out clearly. No fancy language for me, no sir! But now and again I'd come across a poem that spoke to me—usually something kind of morbid—like Yeats's *The Second Coming* or *The Cremation of Sam McGee* by Robert W. Service. Then I joined the Pickups, a band started by my sister Lisa, with guitarist Tony Mandracchia and drummer Tod Tatum. Lisa wrote the words and the music, played bass, and was lead vocalist. I was the backup vocalist and percussionist.

Having no knack for writing poetry/lyrics—I wrote one song, which started like this: "I want to be a zombie, gon' join da living dead. I want to be a zombie, don't shoot me in da head."—I could only sit back and admire her songwriting ability. Her lyrics resonated in a way that most poetry did not, partly because her voice and the instrumental arrangement made the words (sorry) sing. I love all of her songs, but my favorite is "Ghost Road," which Lisa used to introduce at gigs as being a song about "depression and condominiums." We grew up in San Diego and saw much of the open land of our youth built up into malls and condos, so this made sense to me.

For me, however, the song is also about change, good and bad, and the need to let go of the past. The line that gets me every time, that actually makes me tear up whenever I listen to the CD, is this one:

Gotta watch the road ahead I can't keep looking back...

"Erlkönig"
by Johann Wolfgang
von Goethe

Selected and with Commentary
by Nancy Holder

(AKA The Erl-King)

1.
Who rides there so late through the night dark and drear?
The father it is, with his infant so dear;
He holdeth the boy tightly clasp'd in his arm,
He holdeth him safely, he keepeth him warm.

"My son, wherefore seek'st thou thy face thus to hide?"
"Look, father, the Erl-King is close by our side!
Dost see not the Erl-King, with crown and with train?"
"My son, 'tis the mist rising over the plain."

"Oh, come, thou dear infant! oh come thou with me!
Full many a game I will play there with thee;
On my strand, lovely flowers their blossoms unfold,
My mother shall grace thee with garments of gold."

"My father, my father, and dost thou not hear
The words that the Erl-King now breathes in mine ear?"
"Be calm, dearest child, 'tis thy fancy deceives;
'Tis the sad wind that sighs through the withering leaves."

"Wilt go, then, dear infant, wilt go with me there?
My daughters shall tend thee with sisterly care;
My daughters by night their glad festival keep,
They'll dance thee, and rock thee, and sing thee to sleep."

"My father, my father, and dost thou not see,
How the Erl-King his daughters has brought here for me?"
"My darling, my darling, I see it aright,
'Tis the aged grey willows deceiving thy sight."

"I love thee, I'm charm'd by thy beauty, dear boy!
And if thou'rt unwilling, then force I'll employ."
"My father, my father, he seizes me fast,
Full sorely the Erl-King has hurt me at last."

The father now gallops, with terror half wild,
He grasps in his arms the poor shuddering child;
He reaches his courtyard with toil and with dread,—
The child in his arms finds he motionless, dead.

Observations

"Erlkönig" or "The Erl-King" by Johann Wolfgang von Goethe, was written in 1782. Several composers including Franz Schubert set the poem to music. A little boy rides on horseback through a dark and gloomy night with his father. The dreaded Elf King, attracted to the boy, pursues the boy, and attempts to lure him into accompanying him to Elfland by promising fine clothes and dainties; his mother and daughters will attend to the child's every need. The boy tells his father, but the father rationalizes the visitation as natural phenomena: rising mist, dry leaves, shimmering willows. The little boy becomes more and more frantic, shrieking in fear, begging his father to believe him, as the infuriated Elf King moves from wooing him to threatening to take him by force. The father continues to deny all evidence of the supernatural until it is too late—he arrives at their destination with his child dead in his arms.

I have loved the Schubert version since I was very young. I didn't speak German when I first heard it, but Schubert's music celebrates the universal language of growing terror with each stanza.

About Nancy Holder

Nancy Holder is a *New York Times* bestselling author. She is a recipient of seven Bram Stoker Awards, including the Lifetime Achievement Award from the Horror Writers Association. She was also honored with the Faust Grand Master Award by the International Association of Media Tie-in

Writers. An avid Sherlockian, she is a Baker Street Irregular. She is currently serving as coeditor of *The Blue John Gap Project* with her coeditor, Margie Deck, for the Arthur Conan Doyle Society. She is writing two supernatural comic books/graphic novel series, *Johnny Fade* (Moonstone) and *They Call Me Midnight* (IPI Comics) with her writing partner, Alan Philipson.

"THE FAIRIES"
BY WILLIAM ALLINGHAM
Selected and with Commentary
by Jacopo della Quercia

Up the airy mountain,
Down the rushy glen,
We daren't go a hunting
For fear of little men;
Wee folk, good folk,
Trooping all together;
Green jacket, red cap,
And white owl's feather!

Down along the rocky shore
Some make their home,
They live on crispy pancakes
Of yellow tide-foam;
Some in the reeds
Of the black mountain-lake,
With frogs for their watch-dogs,
All night awake.

High on the hill-top
The old King sits;
He is now so old and gray
He's nigh lost his wits.
With a bridge of white mist
Columbkill he crosses,
On his stately journeys
From Slieveleague to Rosses;
Or going up with music
On cold starry nights,

To sup with the Queen
Of the gay Northern Lights.

They stole little Bridget
For seven years long;
When she came down again
Her friends were all gone.
They took her lightly back,
Between the night and morrow,
They thought that she was fast asleep,
But she was dead with sorrow.
They have kept her ever since
Deep within the lakes,
On a bed of flag-leaves,
Watching till she wakes.

By the craggy hill-side,
Through the mosses bare,
They have planted thorn-trees
For pleasure here and there.
Is any man so daring
To dig one up in spite,
He shall find the thorniest set
In his bed at night.

Up the airy mountain,
Down the rushy glen,
We daren't go a hunting
For fear of little men;
Wee folk, good folk,
Trooping all together;
Green jacket, red cap,
And white owl's feather!

OBSERVATIONS

William Butler Yeats described William Allingham in 1891 as "at once the most delicate and the least read" Irish poet. His writings typified how many Irishmen cherished their hometowns and "the mountains they saw from the doors they passed through in childhood." Allingham's most famous verse, "The Fairies," was first published in 1850. The work was immediately praised and shared, albeit with criticisms of the song's poetic meter in *Fraser's Magazine*. The text shown here is how "The Fairies" later appeared in *The Music Master, a Love Story* and *Two Series of Day and Night Songs*. This 1855 reprint featured several departures from the original, most notably its "white owl's feather" instead of "gray-cock's feather" in the first and sixth stanzas.

Despite its prior history, the prominence of "The Fairies" in the 1971 film *Willy Wonka & the Chocolate Factory* cemented it for modern audiences as a work of horror. Its first four lines are quoted early into the film by the "Tinker," a mysterious character created for the movie and described in Roald Dahl's screenplay as "not quite of this world." The name and purpose of this character are never stated, but his ominous use of "The Fairies" primes viewers for the wonders and the terrors inside the factory, which we later learn is staffed with "little men."

Contemporaries fancied fairies both in the real world and in the larger realm of pure imagination.

About Jacopo della Quercia

Jacopo della Quercia is a scholar with Humanities New York, the New York State branch of the National Endowment for the Humanities. He is also the author of several books, among them *License to Quill* and *The Great Abraham Lincoln Pocket Watch Conspiracy*.

"The Giaour"
by George Gordon,
Lord Byron
Selected and with Commentary
by Leslie S. Klinger

(an excerpt of a longer work)

But first, on earth as vampire sent,
Thy corse shall from its tomb be rent:
Then ghastly haunt thy native place,
And suck the blood of all thy race;
There from thy daughter, sister, wife,
At midnight drain the stream of life;
Yet loathe the banquet which perforce
Must feed thy livid living corse:
Thy victims ere they yet expire
Shall know the demon for their sire,
As cursing thee, thou cursing them,
Thy flowers are withered on the stem.
But one that for thy crime must fall,
The youngest, most beloved of all,
Shall bless thee with a father's name—
That word shall wrap thy heart in flame!
Yet must thou end thy task, and mark
Her cheek's last tinge, her eye's last spark,
And the last glassy glance must view
Which freezes o'er its lifeless blue;
Then with unhallowed hand shalt tear
The tresses of her yellow hair,
Of which in life a lock when shorn
Affection's fondest pledge was worn,
But now is borne away by thee,
Memorial of thine agony!

Wet with thine own best blood shall drip
Thy gnashing tooth and haggard lip;
Then stalking to thy sullen grave,
Go—and with Gouls and Afrits rave;
Till these in horror shrink away
From spectre more accursed than they!

Observations

The previous is an excerpt from *The Giaour*, a poem by George Gordon, Lord Byron, first published in 1813. A "giaour" is an infidel, and the poem recounts a tragic tale of a young woman who loved the infidel. It reflects Byron's learning of certain Turkish customs while on a tour of the Continent between 1810 and 1811. Byron was later indirectly involved in the seminal vampire tale *The Vampyre* (1819) written by his friend John Polidori (and initially incorrectly attributed to Byron himself) and is said to have been the model for Lord Ruthven, the titular vampire.

I've long been fascinated by the lore of vampires and the different imaginings of why vampires come into existence. Modern writers have considered vampirism as a disease, an evolutionary experiment, or a demonic possession (to give just a few theories). Here, Byron describes vampirism as the most horrible of curses—to not only suffer the torture of watching one's family die but to be forced to be the source of that torture and death.

About Leslie S. Klinger

Leslie S. Klinger is the editor of the highly acclaimed *The New Annotated Dracula*, *The New Annotated Frankenstein*, and the two-volume *The New Annotated H.P. Lovecraft* as well as the anthologies *In the Shadow of Dracula* and *In the Shadow of Edgar Allan Poe*, featuring 19th-century supernatural fiction. Together with Lisa Morton, he's also edited the anthologies *Ghost Stories Weird Women*, *Weird Women II*, and *Haunted Tales*, all with extensive selections of Victorian horror. He coedited (with Eric Guignard) the Horror Writer's Association's eight-volume *Haunted Library of Horror Classics* and an edition of *Phantasmagoriana*. His latest book is *The New Annotated Strange Case of Dr. Jekyll and Mr. Hyde*.

"The Grave of the Slave"
by Sarah Louise Forten
Selected and with Commentary
by Victor LaValle

The cold storms of winter shall chill him no more,
His woes and his sorrows, his pains are all o'er;
The sod of the valley now covers his form,
He is safe in his last home, he feels not the storm.
The poor slave is laid all unheeded and lone,
Where the rich and the poor find a permanent home;
Not his master can rouse him with voice of command;
He knows not and hears not his cruel demand;
Not a tear, nor a sigh to embalm his cold tomb,
No friend to lament him, no child to bemoan;
Not a stone marks the place where he peacefully lies,
The earth for the pillow, his curtain the skies.
Poor slave, shall we sorrow that death was thy friend,
The last and the kindest that heaven could send?
The grave of the weary is welcomed and blest;
And death to the captive is freedom and rest.

Observations

In certain corners, there are people who work hard to say that slavery *wasn't that bad*. They focus on the "good" slave masters, trying to suggest that while there were a handful of "bad apples," slave masters who were cruel and torturous, there were still many who were loving and kind and only wanted the best for the African Americans they enslaved. This is a lie.

One of the reasons I love this poem so much is because the poet, Sarah Forten Purvis, a Black woman abolitionist from Philadelphia, leaves no room for misinterpretation. For the slave in America there is only one way to find relief: the grave.

While countless poems discuss death as something to fear, Forten chooses to play on a reader's assumptions but using terms like "freedom and rest," or "safe in his last home." This is a powerful use of irony. Without having to state that slavery is evil, she suggests as much, because what kind of life could be so terrible that death would be welcomed? The life of a human held in slavery.

About Victor LaValle

Victor LaValle is the author of eight works of fiction and two graphic novels. His stories, essays, and reviews have been published in *The New York Times*, *The New Yorker*, *The Washington Post*, *GQ*, and many others. His novel, *The Changeling*, has been adapted for television on Apple TV. He has been the recipient of numerous awards, including a World Fantasy, Bram Stoker, Shirley Jackson, and many others. He lives in the Bronx, NY, with his wife and two kids. He teaches writing at Columbia University.

"The Highwayman"
by Alfred Noyes

Selected and with Commentary by Angela Yuriko Smith

The wind was a torrent of darkness among the gusty trees.
The moon was a ghostly galleon tossed upon cloudy seas.
The road was a ribbon of moonlight over the purple moor,
And the highwayman came riding—
Riding—riding—
The highwayman came riding, up to the old inn-door.

He'd a French cocked-hat on his forehead, a bunch of lace at his chin,
A coat of the claret velvet, and breeches of brown doe-skin.
They fitted with never a wrinkle. His boots were up to the thigh.
And he rode with a jewelled twinkle,
His pistol butts a-twinkle,
His rapier hilt a-twinkle, under the jewelled sky.

Over the cobbles he clattered and clashed in the dark inn-yard.
He tapped with his whip on the shutters, but all was locked and barred.
He whistled a tune to the window, and who should be waiting there
But the landlord's black-eyed daughter,
Bess, the landlord's daughter,
Plaiting a dark red love-knot into her long black hair.

And dark in the dark old inn-yard a stable-wicket creaked

Where Tim the ostler listened. His face was white and
    peaked.
His eyes were hollows of madness, his hair like mouldy hay,
But he loved the landlord's daughter,
The landlord's red-lipped daughter.
Dumb as a dog he listened, and he heard the robber say—

"One kiss, my bonny sweetheart, I'm after a prize to-night,
But I shall be back with the yellow gold before the morning
    light;
Yet, if they press me sharply, and harry me through the day,
Then look for me by moonlight,
Watch for me by moonlight,
I'll come to thee by moonlight, though hell should bar the
    way."

He rose upright in the stirrups. He scarce could reach her
    hand,
But she loosened her hair in the casement. His face burnt
    like a brand
As the black cascade of perfume came tumbling over his
    breast;
And he kissed its waves in the moonlight,
(O, sweet black waves in the moonlight!)
Then he tugged at his rein in the moonlight, and galloped
    away to the west.

He did not come in the dawning. He did not come at noon;
And out of the tawny sunset, before the rise of the moon,
When the road was a gypsy's ribbon, looping the purple
    moor,
A red-coat troop came marching—
Marching—marching—
King George's men came marching, up to the old inn-door.

They said no word to the landlord. They drank his ale
    instead.
But they gagged his daughter, and bound her, to the foot of
    her narrow bed.
Two of them knelt at her casement, with muskets at their
    side!
There was death at every window;
And hell at one dark window;
For Bess could see, through her casement, the road that he
    would ride.

They had tied her up to attention, with many a sniggering
    jest.
They had bound a musket beside her, with the muzzle
    beneath her breast!
"Now, keep good watch!" and they kissed her. She heard the
    doomed man say—
Look for me by moonlight;
Watch for me by moonlight;
I'll come to thee by moonlight, though hell should bar
    the way!

She twisted her hands behind her; but all the knots held
    good!
She writhed her hands till her fingers were wet with sweat or
    blood!
They stretched and strained in the darkness, and the hours
    crawled by like years
Till, now, on the stroke of midnight,
Cold, on the stroke of midnight,
The tip of one finger touched it! The trigger at least was
    hers!
The tip of one finger touched it. She strove no more for the
    rest.

Up, she stood up to attention, with the muzzle beneath her
    breast.
She would not risk their hearing; she would not strive again;
For the road lay bare in the moonlight;
Blank and bare in the moonlight;
And the blood of her veins, in the moonlight, throbbed to
    her love's refrain.

Tlot-tlot; tlot-tlot! Had they heard it? The horsehoofs
    ringing clear;
Tlot-tlot; tlot-tlot, in the distance? Were they deaf that they
    did not hear?
Down the ribbon of moonlight, over the brow of the hill,
The highwayman came riding—
Riding—riding—
The red coats looked to their priming! She stood up,
    straight and still.

Tlot-tlot, in the frosty silence! Tlot-tlot, in the echoing
    night!
Nearer he came and nearer. Her face was like a light.

Her eyes grew wide for a moment; she drew one last deep
    breath,
Then her finger moved in the moonlight,
Her musket shattered the moonlight,
Shattered her breast in the moonlight and warned him—
    with her death.

He turned. He spurred to the west; he did not know who
    stood
Bowed, with her head o'er the musket, drenched with her
    own blood!
Not till the dawn he heard it, and his face grew grey to hear
How Bess, the landlord's daughter,
The landlord's black-eyed daughter,
Had watched for her love in the moonlight, and died in the
    darkness there.

Back, he spurred like a madman, shrieking a curse to
    the sky,
With the white road smoking behind him and his rapier
    brandished high.
Blood red were his spurs in the golden noon; wine-red was
    his velvet coat;
When they shot him down on the highway,
Down like a dog on the highway,
And he lay in his blood on the highway, with a bunch of
    lace at his throat.

And still of a winter's night, they say, when the wind is in
    the trees,
When the moon is a ghostly galleon tossed upon cloudy
    seas,
When the road is a ribbon of moonlight over the purple
    moor,
A highwayman comes riding—
Riding—riding—
A highwayman comes riding, up to the old inn-door.

Over the cobbles he clatters and clangs in the dark inn-yard.
He taps with his whip on the shutters, but all is locked and
    barred.
He whistles a tune to the window, and who should be
    waiting there
But the landlord's black-eyed daughter,
Bess, the landlord's daughter,

Plaiting a dark red love-knot into her long black hair.

Observations

"The Highwayman" by Alfred Noyes began my love affair with poetry. I was in second grade in Cheyenne, Wyoming, and it was recess. As usual, all my classmates were off playing games I didn't understand so I went off with a book. I was always reading, but I don't think I'd ever read a poem before. From the first image of the dashing highwayman riding through "a torrent of darkness among the gusty trees" I was hooked. The dusty, midwestern playground evaporated in the heat from this tragic story of Bess, the landlord's beautiful daughter, and the blood sacrifices between two people just trying to be in love. Betrayal, murder, ghosts, a man in lace ... "The Highwayman" had it all.

More than the story, though, this poem opened my mind to what words could be if I let them. Alfred Noyes could have just given me a poem set under a full moon on a windy night, but I probably wouldn't remember this poem some forty years later. Instead, he gave me the moon as "a ghostly galleon tossed upon cloudy seas." The concept of metaphor took my breath away. Suddenly, I understood how magic works. The lovers in the poem were forever doomed, but my own romance with the intoxicating power of poetry had just begun.

About Angela Yuriko Smith

Angela Yuriko Smith is a third-generation Shimanchu/Ryukyuan American, award-winning poet, author, and publisher with more than twenty plus years of newspaper experience. Publisher of *Space & Time* magazine (est. 1966), two-time Bram Stoker Awards Winner, and an Horror Writer's Association Mentor of the Year, she shares *Authortunities*, a free weekly calendar of author opportunities at authortunities.substack.

"The Hollow Men"
by T.S. Eliot
Selected and with Commentary
by James Aquilone

Mistah Kurtz—he dead.
A penny for the Old Guy

I

We are the hollow men
We are the stuffed men
Leaning together
Headpiece filled with straw. Alas!
Our dried voices, when
We whisper together
Are quiet and meaningless
As wind in dry grass
Or rats' feet over broken glass
In our dry cellar
Shape without form, shade without colour,
Paralysed force, gesture without motion;
Those who have crossed
With direct eyes, to death's other Kingdom
Remember us—if at all—not as lost
Violent souls, but only
As the hollow men
The stuffed men.

II

Eyes I dare not meet in dreams
In death's dream kingdom
These do not appear:
There, the eyes are
Sunlight on a broken column
There, is a tree swinging
And voices are
In the wind's singing
More distant and more solemn
Than a fading star.
Let me be no nearer
In death's dream kingdom
Let me also wear
Such deliberate disguises
Rat's coat, crowskin, crossed staves
In a field
Behaving as the wind behaves
No nearer—
Not that final meeting
In the twilight kingdom

III

This is the dead land
This is cactus land
Here the stone images
Are raised, here they receive
The supplication of a dead man's hand
Under the twinkle of a fading star.
Is it like this
In death's other kingdom
Waking alone
At the hour when we are
Trembling with tenderness
Lips that would kiss
Form prayers to broken stone.

IV

The eyes are not here
There are no eyes here
In this valley of dying stars
In this hollow valley
This broken jaw of our lost kingdoms.
In this last of meeting places

We grope together
And avoid speech
Gathered on this beach of the tumid river.
Sightless, unless
The eyes reappear
As the perpetual star
Multifoliate rose
Of death's twilight kingdom
The hope only
Of empty men.

V

Here we go round the prickly pear
Prickly pear prickly pear
Here we go round the prickly pear
At five o'clock in the morning.
Between the idea
And the reality
Between the motion
And the act
Falls the Shadow
For Thine is the Kingdom
Between the conception
And the creation
Between the emotion
And the response
Falls the Shadow
Life is very long
Between the desire
And the spasm
Between the potency
And the existence
Between the essence
And the descent
Falls the Shadow
For Thine is the Kingdom
For Thine is
Life is
For Thine is the
This is the way the world ends
This is the way the world ends
This is the way the world ends
Not with a bang but a whimper.

Observations

Published in 1925, "The Hollow Men" by T.S. Eliot is a poem about hopelessness, apathy, and sterility, a spiritual wasteland. It's filled with esoteric allusions and grim imagery. The language shifts and fragments, reflecting the disillusionment of the post-World War I period.

This was all lost on me as a teen reading a slim volume of T.S. Eliot's collected poems way back when. The references to Dante's *Inferno* and Shakespeare and *The Heart of Darkness* flew over my head. I probably didn't even have a clue about the poem's historical connection to the era. But that didn't affect my appreciation for the work because it made me *feel* Eliot's themes of death, despair, futility, and spiritual emptiness. The essence of the poem burns bright in its language. Lines that continue to echo in my head decades later ... "We are the hollow men / We are the stuffed men" ... "rats' feet over broken glass" ... "death's dream kingdom" ... "In this valley of dying stars," and of course the iconic final lines, which are among the most haunting and quoted of any poet.

Alas, the empty men, headpiece filled with straw, are still leaning together and just as relevant today in a world that seems always on the brink of ending.

About James Aquilone

James Aquilone is an award-winning editor, writer, and publisher. He edited the anthologies *Classic Monsters Unleashed* and *Shakespeare Unleashed*, and *Kolchak: The Night Stalker, 50th Anniversary* graphic novel. He owns Monstrous Books and has won the Bram Stoker Award for Best Graphic Novel, two Rondo Hatton Classic Horror Awards, and a Scribe Award. He lives in Staten Island, New York with his wife, Jennifer.

"The Lady of Shalott"
by Alfred Lord Tennyson
Selected and with Commentary by Paul Cornell

(Original 1832 Version)

Part I
On either side the river lie
Long fields of barley and of rye,
That clothe the wold and meet the sky;
And thro' the field the road runs by
To many-tower'd Camelot;
The yellow-leaved waterlily
The green-sheathed daffodilly
Tremble in the water chilly
Round about Shalott.

Willows whiten, aspens shiver.
The sunbeam showers break and quiver
In the stream that runneth ever
By the island in the river
Flowing down to Camelot.
Four gray walls, and four gray towers
Overlook a space of flowers,
And the silent isle imbowers
The Lady of Shalott.

Underneath the bearded barley,
The reaper, reaping late and early,

Hears her ever chanting cheerly,
Like an angel, singing clearly,
O'er the stream of Camelot.
Piling the sheaves in furrows airy,
Beneath the moon, the reaper weary
Listening whispers, ''Tis the fairy,
Lady of Shalott.'

The little isle is all inrail'd
With a rose-fence, and overtrail'd
With roses: by the marge unhail'd
The shallop flitteth silken sail'd,
Skimming down to Camelot.
A pearl garland winds her head:
She leaneth on a velvet bed,
Full royally apparelled,
The Lady of Shalott.

Part II
No time hath she to sport and play:
A charmed web she weaves alway.
A curse is on her, if she stay
Her weaving, either night or day,
To look down to Camelot.
She knows not what the curse may be;
Therefore she weaveth steadily,
Therefore no other care hath she,
The Lady of Shalott.

She lives with little joy or fear.
Over the water, running near,
The sheepbell tinkles in her ear.
Before her hangs a mirror clear,
Reflecting tower'd Camelot.
And as the mazy web she whirls,
She sees the surly village churls,
And the red cloaks of market girls
Pass onward from Shalott.

Sometimes a troop of damsels glad,
An abbot on an ambling pad,
Sometimes a curly shepherd lad,
Or long-hair'd page in crimson clad,
Goes by to tower'd Camelot:
And sometimes thro' the mirror blue

The knights come riding two and two:
She hath no loyal knight and true,
The Lady of Shalott.

But in her web she still delights
To weave the mirror's magic sights,
For often thro' the silent nights
A funeral, with plumes and lights
And music, came from Camelot:
Or when the moon was overhead
Came two young lovers lately wed;
'I am half sick of shadows,' said
The Lady of Shalott.

Part III
A bow-shot from her bower-eaves,
He rode between the barley-sheaves,
The sun came dazzling thro' the leaves,
And flam'd upon the brazen greaves
Of bold Sir Lancelot.
A red-cross knight for ever kneel'd
To a lady in his shield,
That sparkled on the yellow field,
Beside remote Shalott.

The gemmy bridle glitter'd free,
Like to some branch of stars we see
Hung in the golden Galaxy.
The bridle bells rang merrily
As he rode down from Camelot:
And from his blazon'd baldric slung
A mighty silver bugle hung,
And as he rode his armour rung,
Beside remote Shalott.

All in the blue unclouded weather
Thick-jewell'd shone the saddle-leather,
The helmet and the helmet-feather
Burn'd like one burning flame together,
As he rode down from Camelot.
As often thro' the purple night,
Below the starry clusters bright,
Some bearded meteor, trailing light,
Moves over green Shalott.

His broad clear brow in sunlight glow'd;
On burnish'd hooves his war-horse trode;
From underneath his helmet flow'd
His coal-black curls as on he rode,
As he rode down from Camelot.
From the bank and from the river
He flash'd into the crystal mirror,
'Tirra lirra, tirra lirra:'
Sang Sir Lancelot.

She left the web, she left the loom
She made three paces thro' the room
She saw the water-flower bloom,
She saw the helmet and the plume,
She look'd down to Camelot.
Out flew the web and floated wide;
The mirror crack'd from side to side;
'The curse is come upon me,' cried
The Lady of Shalott.

Part IV
In the stormy east-wind straining,
The pale yellow woods were waning,
The broad stream in his banks complaining,
Heavily the low sky raining
Over tower'd Camelot;
Outside the isle a shallow boat
Beneath a willow lay afloat,
Below the carven stern she wrote,
The Lady of Shalott.

A cloudwhite crown of pearl she dight,
All raimented in snowy white
That loosely flew (her zone in sight
Clasp'd with one blinding diamond bright)
Her wide eyes fix'd on Camelot,
Though the squally east-wind keenly
Blew, with folded arms serenely
By the water stood the queenly
Lady of Shalott.

With a steady stony glance—
Like some bold seer in a trance,
Beholding all his own mischance,
Mute, with a glassy countenance—

She look'd down to Camelot.
It was the closing of the day:
She loos'd the chain, and down she lay;
The broad stream bore her far away,
  The Lady of Shalott.

As when to sailors while they roam,
By creeks and outfalls far from home,
Rising and dropping with the foam,
From dying swans wild warblings come,
  Blown shoreward; so to Camelot
Still as the boathead wound along
The willowy hills and fields among,
They heard her chanting her deathsong,
  The Lady of Shalott.

A longdrawn carol, mournful, holy,
She chanted loudly, chanted lowly,
Till her eyes were darken'd wholly,
And her smooth face sharpen'd slowly,
  Turn'd to tower'd Camelot:
For ere she reach'd upon the tide
The first house by the water-side,
Singing in her song she died,
  The Lady of Shalott.

Under tower and balcony,
By garden wall and gallery,
A pale, pale corpse she floated by,
Deadcold, between the houses high,
  Dead into tower'd Camelot.
Knight and burgher, lord and dame,
To the planked wharfage came:
Below the stern they read her name,
  The Lady of Shalott.

They cross'd themselves, their stars they blest,
Knight, minstrel, abbot, squire, and guest.
There lay a parchment on her breast,
That puzzled more than all the rest,
  The wellfed wits at Camelot.
'The web was woven curiously,
The charm is broken utterly,
Draw near and fear not,—this is I,
  The Lady of Shalott.'

Observations

I've always loved how Arthurian works tend to focus on side quests, how Camelot is over there, but our main story is over here. (A feature summed up pithily by Monty Python.) In "The Lady of Shalott" we're with an isolated royal figure, possibly a fairy, in her tower, looking at her mirror while she weaves a "charmed web." She's cursed to only see the splendour of Camelot in reflection. If she stops weaving and turns to look at the reality, something terrible will happen. There's something deep and only vaguely defined going on here at both a psychological and cosmic level. Is she weaving the passage of time, like one of the Fates? If she goes to participate in it, then it breaks. If she observes it, dare we say the waveform collapses? Maybe this is the creative person's lot, to describe but not to take part in the passing parade. Jasper Fforde has the mirror being a way for fictional characters to observe the real.

At any rate, seeing Sir Lancelot going past finally ruins her composure. She turns to look and *ka-boom!* "Out flew the web and floated wide/the mirror crack'd from side to side." (One of the many gifts to subsequent fiction in this poem.) She gets into a boat, and heads for Camelot, but, and one senses she knows this is how it's going to go, she doesn't make it. The knights hear her "deathsong," and when she gets to their castle she's already dead, leaving only an identifying note. The poem makes a slight dig at the "wellfed wits of Camelot" who don't understand what they're looking at. And it must be said, in a very male way, they've managed to completely ignore this burdened, hard-working woman on their doorstep, whose death was probably down to her Lancelot fandom.

The poem influenced many visual artists, notably the Pre-Raphaelites, John William Waterhouse and William Holman Hunt, both producing memorable paintings of the subject. Myself, I'd say that though some of the heartfelt rhyming can seem silly to the modern ear, there's still a mysterious power to the piece, which I think stems from its ambiguity, its ability to describe both our immediate psyches and the whole texture of reality at once. It's odd to say about a piece of Arthuriana, but to me "The Lady of Shalott" feels extraordinarily real.

About Paul Cornell

Paul Cornell has written episodes of *Elementary*, *Doctor Who* ("Father's Day" and "Human Nature"), *Primeval*, *Robin Hood*, and many other TV series, including his own ITV children's show, *Wavelength*. He's worked for every major comics company, including his creator-owned series *I Walk With Monsters* for Vault Comics, *The Modern Frankenstein* for Magma, *Saucer Country* for Vertigo, and *This Damned Band* for Dark Horse, and runs for Marvel and DC on *Batman and Robin*, *Wolverine*, and *Young Avengers*. He's the writer of the Lychford rural fantasy novellas from Tor.com Publishing (now *Reactor Magazine*). He's won the BSFA Award for his short fiction, an Eagle Award for his comics, a Hugo Award for his podcast, and shares in a Writer's Guild Award for his *Doctor Who* episodes and the Grand Prix Nova and Scribe awards for the audio series, *Tom Clancy's Splinter Cell: Firewall*. He's the co-host of *Hammer House of Podcast*. His latest book is the SF novella *Rosebud*, his latest graphic novel is *The Witches of World War II* for TKO, and his latest comic series is *Con and On* for Ahoy.

"The Little Ghost"
by Edna St. Vincent Millay
Selected and with Commentary
by Stephanie M. Wytovich

I knew her for a little ghost
That in my garden walked;
The wall is high—higher than most—
And the green gate was locked.

And yet I did not think of that
Till after she was gone—
I knew her by the broad white hat,
All ruffled, she had on.

By the dear ruffles round her feet,
By her small hands that hung
In their lace mitts, austere and sweet,
Her gown's white folds among.

I watched to see if she would stay,
What she would do—and oh!
She looked as if she liked the way
I let my garden grow!

She bent above my favourite mint
With conscious garden grace,
She smiled and smiled—there was no hint
Of sadness in her face.

She held her gown on either side

To let her slippers show,
And up the walk she went with pride,
The way great ladies go.

And where the wall is built in new
And is of ivy bare
She paused—then opened and passed through
A gate that once was there.

Observations

When it comes to speculative poetry, it doesn't always have to be about the jump scare or the gore. Hauntings and horror come in all shapes and sizes, and something I love about Edna St. Vincent Millay's piece "The Little Ghost" is that it's a snapshot of a day in the afterlife, a small ethereal glimpse at a dead child walking amongst the ivy. That said, it's not sad and it doesn't aim to terrify or torment, but rather to hint at the spectral whimsy of a ghost. Here we have a little girl in a white dress admiring the garden and taking in the fresh bite of mint, a smile on her face.

This is a ghost story, yes, but it's also a story about ghosts, about how there can still be joy and peace on the other side, how we live in an extended state of liminality, and how even after death, little girls can frolic amongst the flowers in their favorite dresses, choosing when and where to open the next gate, pick the next flower, and cheekily grin at an unsuspecting gardener as they slip behind the veil. This is horror, but it's also a poem about hope, and it's important to remember that you often can't have one without the other.

About Stephanie M. Wytovich

Stephanie M. Wytovich is an American poet, novelist, and essayist. She is a recipient of the Elizabeth Matchett Stover Memorial Award, the 2016 Bram Stoker Award, the 2021 Ladies of Horror Fiction Writers Grant, and has received the Rocky Wood Memorial Scholarship for nonfiction writing. Follow Wytovich at stephaniemwytovich.com and on Twitter and Instagram @SWytovich and @thehauntedbookshelf. You can also sign up for her newsletter at stephaniemwytovich.substack.com.

"The March of the Dead"
by Robert Service
Selected and with Commentary
by Christopher Golden

The cruel war was over—oh, the triumph was so sweet!
We watched the troops returning, through our tears;
There was triumph, triumph, triumph down the scarlet
    glittering street,
And you scarce could hear the music for the cheers.
And you scarce could see the house-tops for the flags that
    flew between;
The bells were pealing madly to the sky;
And everyone was shouting for the Soldiers of the Queen,
And the glory of an age was passing by.

And then there came a shadow, swift and sudden, dark and
    drear;
The bells were silent, not an echo stirred.
The flags were drooping sullenly, the men forgot to cheer;
We waited, and we never spoke a word.
The sky grew darker, darker, till from out the gloomy rack
There came a voice that checked the heart with dread:
"Tear down, tear down your bunting now, and hang up
    sable black;
They are coming—it's the Army of the Dead."

They were coming, they were coming, gaunt and ghastly,
    sad and slow;
They were coming, all the crimson wrecks of pride;
With faces seared, and cheeks red smeared, and haunting
    eyes of woe,
And clotted holes the khaki couldn't hide.

Oh, the clammy brow of anguish! the livid, foam-flecked
    lips!
The reeling ranks of ruin swept along!
The limb that trailed, the hand that failed, the bloody finger
    tips!
And oh, the dreary rhythm of their song!

"They left us on the veldt-side, but we felt we couldn't stop
On this, our England's crowning festal day;
We're the men of Magersfontein, we're the men of
    Spion Kop,
Colenso—we're the men who had to pay.
We're the men who paid the blood-price. Shall the grave be
    all our gain?
You owe us. Long and heavy is the score.
Then cheer us for our glory now, and cheer us for our pain,
And cheer us as ye never cheered before."

The folks were white and stricken, and each tongue seemed
    weighted with lead;
Each heart was clutched in hollow hand of ice;
And every eye was staring at the horror of the dead,
The pity of the men who paid the price.
They were come, were come to mock us, in the first flush of
    our peace;
Through writhing lips their teeth were all agleam;
They were coming in their thousands—oh, would they
    never cease!
I closed my eyes, and then—it was a dream.

There was triumph, triumph, triumph down the scarlet
    gleaming street;
The town was mad; a man was like a boy.
A thousand flags were flaming where the sky and city meet;
A thousand bells were thundering the joy.
There was music, mirth and sunshine; but some eyes shone
    with regret;
And while we stun with cheers our homing braves,
O God, in Thy great mercy, let us nevermore forget
The graves they left behind, the bitter graves

Observations

I was first drawn to the works of Robert Service through his poems about daring the frozen wilderness. In my mind, he shared space with Jack London in that regard. Yet, as with London, I discovered there was much more to his imagination than Gold Rush adventures and atavistic survival stories. I encountered "The March of the Dead" in a collection of Service's poetry, and I remember my breath turning shallow. It felt like a bell had rung, and I hadn't even read to the end before I went back to the beginning, to savor it. The cadence, that drum beating the rhythm for the march, helped bring the poem to life. But it was the bait-and-switch of the language that both unsettled me and made me want to cheer. The troops are returning from war. Flags are flying. There are tears of joy to celebrate this glorious homecoming. But then the surviving soldiers are followed by all those who have died on the battlefield, and the horrific cost of the war comes home. It's a shocking turn, that completely changes the tone and purpose of the poem. It's a horror story, an anti-war chant, and—to my mind—a masterpiece.

Many years later, while rewatching *The Twilight Zone*, it occurred to me to wonder if the 1961 episode "The Passersby" had been inspired by "The March of the Dead." In the days immediately following the end of the American Civil War, soldiers marching home along a particular road realize they are all dead. Watch that episode for yourself and see what you think.

A more personal note to share—Service has been my favorite poet since my teen years. Though perhaps unsophisticated, his work is deeply, emotionally resonant. When I was in my thirties, my uncle gave me a packet of letters that my late father had written to his Aunt Marguerite while he was stationed on Kodiak Island, Alaska, during the Korean War, serving with the Coast Guard. Reading through those letters, I learned that his commanding officer had given him a book of poems that had affected him profoundly, and he carried that book around the island with him. Yes, of course. Robert Service. His new favorite poet. My father had been dead more than fifteen years by then, but suddenly we shared something that we never had while he was alive. Those letters were a gift I will always cherish.

About Christopher Golden

Christopher Golden is *The New York Times* bestselling author of such novels as *The House of Last Resort*, *All Hallows*, *Road of Bones*, and the Stoker Award-winning *Ararat*, among many others. Golden co-created (with Mike Mignola) the fan favorite comic book series *Baltimore* and *Joe Golem: Occult Detective*. As an editor, his short story anthologies include *Hex Life*, *Seize the Night*, and *The New Dead*, among others. He has also written and co-written comic books, video games, screenplays, a BBC radio play, and the online animated series *Ghosts of Albion* (with Amber Benson). His work has been nominated for the British Fantasy Award, the Eisner Award, and multiple Shirley Jackson Awards. He has been nominated eleven times in eight different categories for the Bram Stoker Award, and has won twice, including Best Novel. He shared a win in the Shirley Jackson Awards in 2020 for coediting the anthology *The Twisted Book of Shadows* with fellow author and editor James A. Moore. In 2023, Golden and Amber Benson co-wrote and co-directed the Audible Original podcast *Slayers: A Buffyverse Story*. His original novels have been published in countries and languages around the world. For more information, please visit him at christophergolden.com.

"The Mermaid"
by William Butler Yeats
Selected and with Commentary by Laurell K. Hamilton

A mermaid found a swimming lad,
Picked him for her own,
Pressed her body to his body,
Laughed: and plunging down
Forgot in cruel happiness
That even lovers drown.

Observations

Is love ever safe or is it like the ocean so vast and full of mysteries that we never know if the siren that calls to our heart is going to sink our ship and devour us or give us our happily ever after.

For many of us love is followed by abuse or worse, and like the mermaid's lover we drown in the sea of obsessive love. Possession is not love, but abusers don't know the difference. You're mine so I'll take you with me wherever I go even if it kills you.

The mermaid never means to drown you, they just forget that what is life for them may mean death for you. They love you; they want you, and that matters more than how you feel about them. Nowhere in the poem does it say the "swimming lad" wanted the mermaid, but that doesn't matter to monsters looking for their next victim.

About Laurell K. Hamilton

Laurell K. Hamilton is the author of the #1 *New York Times* bestselling Anita Blake, Vampire Hunter series and the Merry Gentry, Fey Detective series. *A Terrible Fall of Angels*, the first novel in an exciting new series, features Detective Zaniel Havelock in a world where angels and demons walk among us. With more than forty novels published, Laurell continues to create groundbreaking fiction inspired by her lifelong love of monster movies, ghost stories, mythology, folklore, and things that go bump in the night. Her love of the macabre, books in general, animals, and nature led her to degrees in English and biology. She is a non-practicing biologist but uses her science to add an extra level of realism to her fiction. She currently lives in St. Louis with her family, a house Lion, and three kittens. In her free time, Laurell trains in Filipino martial arts with a specialization in blade work and travels to scuba dive and bird watch as often as she can.

"The Only Ghost I Ever Saw" by Emily Dickinson

Selected and with Commentary by Anne Walsh

The only ghost I ever saw
Was dressed in mechlin,—so;
He wore no sandal on his foot,
And stepped like flakes of snow.
His gait was soundless, like the bird,
But rapid, like the roe;
His fashions quaint, mosaic,
Or, haply, mistletoe.
His conversation seldom,
His laughter like the breeze
That dies away in dimples
Among the pensive trees.
Our interview was transient,—
Of me, himself was shy;
And God forbid I look behind
Since that appalling day!

Observations

I chose this poem because I love that it feels like Emily Dickinson actually saw this ghost and was scared by the memory of it. I love how the plain and to-the-point title draws us in. We know immediately that we're in a ghost story. And we want to be. And we believe Dickinson because it's the *only* ghost she ever saw. This singular entity is already a force. But the main thing is the thing itself: this poem, this ghost are both hardly there at first— diaphanous entities, floating as if among trees. But they both take a turn.

They become things whose silent glide beside Dickinson is as fast as a deer, and who, by the last four lines, become awful with the idea of a conversation between the poet and the ghost. However short this "interview," it's no less frightening in retrospect to the poet or to the reader. The hair on our neck rises, faster than this deer-quick ghost of the woods, with those last two lines. In them, the ghost is no longer one whose laugh dies away "in dimples among the pensive trees" (scary enough to contemplate). Suddenly, this entity is something that the poet doesn't want to see ever again.

Dickinson spins this poem-ghost-story with her own lightest spectral fingers, with perfect descriptions of this entity as neither here nor there, not much more than a snowflake, a sprig of mistletoe, or the dapple of sun between branches. But she comes down quick with a gavel of horror that says this ghost moves fast and talks. Then bluntly she tells us that she will never look behind her again. Whoa, those last two lines deliver the creep factor better than any others. And that Dickinson waits until the end to deliver this spine-freeze leaves us with her lingering fear to look behind ourselves. Because, of course, such an entity could appear to any of us. In fact, this exact entity could appear to any of us if we contemplate him long enough in her short words. He could speak to us. He could dog us. And he does. He does. So, don't turn around.

I've read that many scholars feel that this poem might be another of Dickinson's "riddle" poems; that the ghost is snow, a tree, or another narrator. Could be. Dickinson wrote riddle poems, and you can easily imagine this ghost as a tree that she's observing with her microscope soul. But I like to feel it as a ghost poem and to let those last four lines climb up my spine like one. Although, if it is a riddle, maybe the ghost in the poem is poetry. After all, this poem itself is a testament to how a poem can haunt you as a reader. And as a poet, well, you can never get away from poetry's inexorable voice or from its pursuit of you every second "... rapid as the roe" —poetry as an entity that *will* speak to you, and that will alter your life with the exchange. Still, this poem is best read to unsuspecting friends by the light of a single candle on Halloween night.

About Anne Walsh

Anne Walsh is a widely published poet in Australia and in the US She's been shortlisted twice for both the Newcastle Poetry Prize and the ACU Prize for literature. In 2020, at the invitation of American actor Tituss Burgess, she read her work as part of Carnegie Hall's inaugural live online concert.

"The Opal Dream Cave"
by Katherine Mansfield
Selected and with Commentary
by Lee Murray

In an opal dream cave I found a fairy:
Her wings were frailer than flower petals—
Frailer far than snowflakes.
She was not frightened, but poised on my finger,
Then delicately walked into my hand.
I shut the two palms of my hands together
And held her prisoner.
I carried her out of the opal cave,
Then opened my hands.
First she became thistledown,
Then a mote in a sunbeam,
Then—nothing at all.
Empty now is my opal dream cave.

Observations

For several years I lived on Tinakori Road on the windy slopes of New Zealand's capital, Wellington, just steps from the elegant weatherboard town house where Katherine Mansfield (or Kathleen Beauchamp) spent her childhood. One of Aotearoa's most acclaimed writers, Mansfield is best known for her sparse yet breathtakingly sharp short stories, many of which captured the "savage spirit" of the country as she called it. As a character, she was something of a rebel, an outspoken, queer young woman with a cantankerous "surly" nature, a feminist chafed by the trappings of society—much to the distress of her parents—and who disdained the pomposity of intellectuals—despite keeping company with some of the most celebrated literati of the day, among them D.H. and Frieda Lawrence and Virginia Woolf.

This tiny single-stanza poem by Mansfield, "The Opal Dream Cave" (1911), was written before the poet contracted pulmonary tuberculosis, for which there was no known cure, so in some ways the verse is prophetic, a dark whisper of the sad destiny that awaited her. After her diagnosis in 1917, Mansfield drifted across Europe, staying in pensions and guest houses, looking for better climate or any treatment which might prolong her life. The poem could also be interpreted as a metaphor for the loss of childhood wonder; her isolation from her beloved New Zealand in her last year, a place which she claimed was "in my very bones"; a reference to the lovechild that Mansfield tragically miscarried; her belief she was a misfit; or perhaps it reflects her disillusionment that her writing would not be "fashionable for long." I like the poem for the simplicity of the text, the immediacy of the first-person approach, and the underlying hint of cruelty that typically accompanies captured fairy or changeling narratives. Mostly, the poem resonates for me for the Pandora's Box moment of possibility, that tenuous tipping point for change. What might happen when the narrator opens her hands? Will she be cursed? Rewarded? In "The Opal Dream Cave" Mansfield reveals how, for her at least, the prospect of fading into nothingness and indifference represents an even worse fate. I explore a similar theme in my own poetry, for example in "fury," a tiny poem which appears in *Tortured Willows: Bent. Bowed. Unbroken.* (a collaborative collection by Asian diaspora horror poets). However, in my poem, the fairy is replaced with the hungry ghost of Chinese mythology:

fury

inside
a man-crafted
box of woman-should
a hungry ghost

I let her out

About Lee Murray

Lee Murray is a multi-award-winning writer, editor, and poet from Aotearoa-New Zealand, and a five-time Bram Stoker Award winner, including for poetry for *Tortured Willows* (with Christina Sng, Angela Yuriko Smith, and Geneve Flynn). She holds New Zealand's Prime Minister's Award for Literary Achievement and is an Honorary Literary Fellow of the New Zealand Society of Authors. While still unpublished, her poetry collection *Fox Spirit on a Distant Cloud* (2024) won her a Grimshaw Sargeson Fellowship and the NZSA Laura Solomon Cuba Press Prize. Her poem "cheongsam" won the 2021 Australian Shadows Award for poetry. She is an Elgin Award runner up, and a Rhysling, Dwarf Star, and Pushcart-nominated poet, and coeditor (with Lindy Ryan) of *Under Her Eye*, a women in horror poetry project for the Pixels Project to eliminate violence against women. Read more at leemurray.info.

Editor's Note

Because poetry, by its nature, is open to endless interpretation, I asked two different creatives to provide observations on one of the true classics—Poe's "The Raven." A poem that I think everyone has read in school or elsewhere, and which is certainly a foundational poem of personal darkness. Below you'll find the full poem along with observations by poet & poetry teacher, Eileen M. D'Angelo, and following her entry will be commentary by actor and audiobook narrator, Scott Brick. An entire book could be filled with multiple takes on the same source poem—or on virtually every poem. So, enjoy the poem and these two entries.

"THE RAVEN"
BY EDGAR ALLAN POE
SELECTED AND WITH COMMENTARY
BY EILEEN M. D'ANGELO

Once upon a midnight dreary, while I pondered, weak and
 weary,
Over many a quaint and curious volume of forgotten lore—
While I nodded, nearly napping, suddenly there came a
 tapping,
As of some one gently rapping, rapping at my chamber
 door.
"'Tis some visitor," I muttered, "tapping at my chamber
 door—
Only this and nothing more."

Ah, distinctly I remember it was in the bleak December;
And each separate dying ember wrought its ghost upon the
 floor.
Eagerly I wished the morrow;—vainly I had sought to
 borrow
From my books surcease of sorrow—sorrow for the lost
 Lenore—
For the rare and radiant maiden whom the angels name
 Lenore—
Nameless here for evermore.

And the silken, sad, uncertain rustling of each purple
 curtain
Thrilled me—filled me with fantastic terrors never felt
 before;
So that now, to still the beating of my heart, I stood
 repeating

"'Tis some visitor entreating entrance at my chamber door—
Some late visitor entreating entrance at my chamber door;
This it is and nothing more."

Presently my soul grew stronger; hesitating then no longer,
"Sir," said I, "or Madam, truly your forgiveness I implore;
But the fact is I was napping, and so gently you came rapping,
And so faintly you came tapping, tapping at my chamber door,
That I scarce was sure I heard you"—here I opened wide the door;—
Darkness there and nothing more.

Deep into that darkness peering, long I stood there wondering, fearing,
Doubting, dreaming dreams no mortal ever dared to dream before;
But the silence was unbroken, and the stillness gave no token,
And the only word there spoken was the whispered word, "Lenore?"
This I whispered, and an echo murmured back the word, "Lenore!"—
Merely this and nothing more.

Back into the chamber turning, all my soul within me burning,
Soon again I heard a tapping somewhat louder than before.
"Surely," said I, "surely that is something at my window lattice;
Let me see, then, what thereat is, and this mystery explore—
Let my heart be still a moment and this mystery explore;—
'Tis the wind and nothing more!"

Open here I flung the shutter, when, with many a flirt and flutter,
In there stepped a stately Raven of the saintly days of yore;
Not the least obeisance made he; not a minute stopped or stayed he;
But, with mien of lord or lady, perched above my chamber door—

Perched upon a bust of Pallas just above my chamber
    door—
Perched, and sat, and nothing more.

Then this ebony bird beguiling my sad fancy into smiling,
By the grave and stern decorum of the countenance it wore,
"Though thy crest be shorn and shaven, thou," I said, "art
    sure no craven,
Ghastly grim and ancient Raven wandering from the
    Nightly shore—
Tell me what thy lordly name is on the Night's Plutonian
    shore!"
Quoth the Raven "Nevermore."

Much I marvelled this ungainly fowl to hear discourse so
    plainly,
Though its answer little meaning—little relevancy bore;
For we cannot help agreeing that no living human being
Ever yet was blessed with seeing bird above his chamber
    door—
Bird or beast upon the sculptured bust above his chamber
    door,
With such name as "Nevermore."

But the Raven, sitting lonely on the placid bust, spoke only
That one word, as if his soul in that one word he did
    outpour.
Nothing farther then he uttered—not a feather then he
    fluttered—
Till I scarcely more than muttered "Other friends have
    flown before—
On the morrow he will leave me, as my Hopes have flown
    before."
Then the bird said "Nevermore."

Startled at the stillness broken by reply so aptly spoken,
"Doubtless," said I, "what it utters is its only stock and store
Caught from some unhappy master whom unmerciful
    Disaster
Followed fast and followed faster till his songs one burden
    bore—
Till the dirges of his Hope that melancholy burden bore
Of 'Never—nevermore'."

But the Raven still beguiling all my fancy into smiling,

Straight I wheeled a cushioned seat in front of bird, and
    bust and door;
Then, upon the velvet sinking, I betook myself to linking
Fancy unto fancy, thinking what this ominous bird of
    yore—
What this grim, ungainly, ghastly, gaunt, and ominous bird
    of yore
Meant in croaking "Nevermore."

This I sat engaged in guessing, but no syllable expressing
To the fowl whose fiery eyes now burned into my bosom's
    core;
This and more I sat divining, with my head at ease reclining
On the cushion's velvet lining that the lamp-light gloated
    o'er,
But whose velvet-violet lining with the lamp-light gloating
    o'er,
She shall press, ah, nevermore!

Then, methought, the air grew denser, perfumed from an
    unseen censer
Swung by Seraphim whose foot-falls tinkled on the tufted
    floor.
"Wretch," I cried, "thy God hath lent thee—by these angels
    he hath sent thee
Respite—respite and nepenthe from thy memories of
    Lenore;
Quaff, oh quaff this kind nepenthe and forget this lost
    Lenore!"
Quoth the Raven "Nevermore."

"Prophet!" said I, "thing of evil!—prophet still, if bird or
    devil!—
Whether Tempter sent, or whether tempest tossed thee here
    ashore,
Desolate yet all undaunted, on this desert land
    enchanted—
On this home by Horror haunted—tell me truly, I
    implore—
Is there—is there balm in Gilead?—tell me—tell me, I
    implore!"
Quoth the Raven "Nevermore."

"Prophet!" said I, "thing of evil!—prophet still, if bird or
    devil!

By that Heaven that bends above us—by that God we both
    adore—
Tell this soul with sorrow laden if, within the distant
    Aidenn,
It shall clasp a sainted maiden whom the angels name
    Lenore—
Clasp a rare and radiant maiden whom the angels name
    Lenore."
Quoth the Raven "Nevermore."

"Be that word our sign of parting, bird or fiend!" I shrieked,
    upstarting—
"Get thee back into the tempest and the Night's Plutonian
    shore!
Leave no black plume as a token of that lie thy soul hath
    spoken!
Leave my loneliness unbroken!—quit the bust above my
    door!
Take thy beak from out my heart, and take thy form from
    off my door!"
Quoth the Raven "Nevermore."

And the Raven, never flitting, still is sitting, still is sitting
On the pallid bust of Pallas just above my chamber door;
And his eyes have all the seeming of a demon's that is
    dreaming,
And the lamp-light o'er him streaming throws his shadow
    on the floor;
And my soul from out that shadow that lies floating on the
    floor
Shall be lifted—nevermore!

OBSERVATIONS

This Gothic literary ballad is one of the most famous and unforgettable poems ever written.

    Narrated by a heartsick lover devastated over the loss of his beloved "Lenore," Poe's classic poem is mysterious and dark, from the entrance of a supernatural bird to the narrator's descent into madness. Let's start with the raven, perched upon the Goddess of Wisdom, Athena, haunting the grief-stricken narrator. Ravens have long been symbols of many things in history from bad omens and prophecy to wisdom; but this raven's presence is a symbol of death and the agony of loss, and love that transcends the grave.

This is no ordinary raven. This bird flies in the window on a stormy night to torment a young man who is grieving. Again and again, the bird's "Nevermore!" pushes the man to the brink of insanity until he curses the raven, is consumed by depression, and has lost all hope. Just as the raven entered his window, suffering has entered his life and will never leave.

A well-crafted masterpiece in trochaic octameter, the poem's complicated structure and rhyme scheme causes a jangling of words like wind chimes and a luscious excess of sounds. The combination of assonance and alliteration creates music, drama, and an intense, mysterious mood. The nuns in Southwest Philly got it right. In Catholic school, nuns would randomly choose students to read each stanza. "The Raven" was written to be read *aloud*, in the oral tradition, to hear the unique musicality and pounding rhythm building tension, fear, and anticipation. Poe aimed for his poems to be approximately one hundred lines in length, and "The Raven" tops in at 108 lines, start to finish. In Poe's era, it was good to be wordy, because publishers paid by the line. Eighteen stanzas from start to chilling finale, this poem is jam-packed with an overwhelming sense of terror and soul-crushing despair, with a twist of the supernatural and the occult. *All this*—and the mystical raven, with his one-word, foreboding refrain.

What's the secret of its timelessness? Not only has this poem wended its way into American pop culture and been parodied countless times with its ghostly imagery and haunting tone; but it's *universal*, and that's the key to the poem's staying power. It spans 179 years with its themes of unending agony, heartbreak, and inconsolable grief. The emotions Poe pounds into us through these words are eternal and human. The universal themes expressed, most notably, *unrelenting anguish over the devastating loss of a loved one*, make this literary ballad as relevant today as it was in 1845—and one of the most memorable poems of all time.

About Eileen M. D'Angelo

Eileen M. D'Angelo, Executive Director of Mad Poets Society, is former Editor of *Mad Poets Review* and has been nominated twice for both a Pennsylvania Governor's Award in the Arts and the Pushcart Prize. D'Angelo's poetry and reviews have been published in *Rattle*, *Manhattan Poetry Review*, *Paterson Literary Review*, *Drexel Online Journal*, *Wild River Review*, the *Philadelphia Inquirer*, *Philadelphia Stories*, and others. She judged open auditions for the pilot program of HBO's / Russell Simmons's *Def Poetry Jam*. She conducted workshops and performed original songs and poetry on WXPN's *World Café*, at the Painted Bride Art Center, South St. Arts Festival, Hedgerow Theatre, St. Joe's, Princeton, and Philly Fringe Festival, among other venues.

"THE RAVEN"
BY EDGAR ALLAN POE
SELECTED AND WITH COMMENTARY
BY SCOTT BRICK

(**Editor's Note:** See previous entry for the full text and a different perspective on this classic)

OBSERVATIONS

"The Raven's rhyme scheme is musical to the point of joviality, yet author Edgar Allan Poe endured perhaps the greatest period of prolonged mourning in history, nearly every day of his adult life. "The Raven"'s rhythm hid the burning sorrow that lies at the heart of Poe's masterpiece. He lost his father, his mother, his brother, his foster-mother, and his wife during his brief forty-year life. It was his mother's loss in 1811 that introduced him to the horrors of tuberculosis, and sadly was the harbinger of the preeminent loss of his life: his wife Virginia Eliza Poe was seen coughing up blood into a handkerchief in 1842. She would die five years later.

Loss lies at the heart of all of Poe's greatest works, especially those written during a brief period: the tuberculosis-inspired "Masque of the Red Death" (1842), "The Raven" (1845), and his last great work, the poem "Annabel Lee" (published after Poe's death in 1849). The inspiration for all of them have been attributed to Eliza's ultimate demise after her diagnosis, but the timing is morbidly fascinating: it's as though he wrote of his wife's loss *before* it occurred; he mourned Eliza before she was gone, as if to prepare himself, knowing he would soon do so again. The loss central to "The Raven" is therefore far more poignant.

Many readers have lamented the fact that Poe died so young, all of them longing for the works he might have written had he lived longer, and I do as well. But I also, when considering the "what might have been" nature of his brief life, ponder what it would have been like to meet the woman who inspired such an extraordinary outpouring of literary masterpieces. I wish I could have known Virginia Eliza Poe. But alas, to quote the central character of Poe's greatest known work: "Nevermore."

About Scott Brick

Scott Brick has narrated bestsellers and Pulitzer Prize winners for every major publisher in every conceivable category, over 1,100 titles, including *Jurassic Park*, *The Hunt for Red October*, *In Cold Blood*, *Bladerunner*, and the entire Dune saga. Scott is both an AudioFile Magazine Golden Voice and an inaugural member of the Audible Narrator Hall of Fame, and in 2015 Scott began teaching the nation's first fully accredited university course in audiobook narration at UCLA.

"The Ruined Chapel"
by William Allingham
Selected and with Commentary
by Tim Lebbon

By the shore, a plot of ground
Clips a ruin'd chapel round,
Buttress'd with a grassy mound;
Where Day and Night and Day go by
And bring no touch of human sound.

Washing of the lonely seas,
Shaking of the guardian trees,
Piping of the salted breeze;
Day and Night and Day go by
To the endless tune of these.

Or when, as winds and waters keep
A hush more dead than any sleep,
Still morns to stiller evenings creep,
And Day and Night and Day go by;
Here the silence is most deep.

The empty ruins, lapsed again
Into Nature's wide domain,
Sow themselves with seed and grain
As Day and Night and Day go by;
And hoard June's sun and April's rain.

Here fresh funeral tears were shed;
Now the graves are also dead;
And suckers from the ash-tree spread,
While Day and Night and Day go by;

And stars move calmly overhead.

Observations

There's something melancholy and sad about "The Ruined Chapel," but also something quite beautiful. It describes a human place where no more humans dwell. Where "the graves are also dead" where once "fresh funeral tears were shed." And that's also quite chilling because it suggests that humanity isn't really needed at all. Day and night and day go by, again and again, and the only change to this timeless scene is the wash of water or the kiss of a sea breeze.

We know this, of course. We're mere guests here, and whatever songs or silences haunt this desolate ruin will sing or pause whether people are present to hear and experience them, or not. There's also the sense that this old chapel will slowly succumb to time and will be taken down once again into "Nature's wide domain." It's a remnant of a time gone by, a motionless monument to the busy people who built it, and prayed, and were buried here.

And I think that's why this poem sings to me. More than anything, it resounds with the beauty, power, and timelessness of nature all around us, and brings home the fact that our time here is but a blink between eons.

About Tim Lebbon

Tim Lebbon is a *New York Times* bestselling writer from South Wales. He's had over forty novels published to date, as well as hundreds of novellas and short stories, scripts, and comics. His latest novel is *Among The Living*. He has won a World Fantasy Award and four British Fantasy Awards, as well as Bram Stoker, Scribe, and Dragon Awards.

The movie of his novel *The Silence* debuted on Netflix in April 2019, and *Pay the Ghost* was released Halloween 2015. Tim is currently developing more novels, short stories, audio dramas, and projects for TV and the big screen. Find out more: timlebbon.net.

"The Second Coming"
by W.B. Yeats
Selected and with Commentary
by Craig Engler

Turning and turning in the widening gyre
The falcon cannot hear the falconer;
Things fall apart; the centre cannot hold;
Mere anarchy is loosed upon the world,
The blood-dimmed tide is loosed, and everywhere
The ceremony of innocence is drowned;
The best lack all conviction, while the worst
Are full of passionate intensity.
Surely some revelation is at hand;
Surely the Second Coming is at hand.
The Second Coming! Hardly are those words out
When a vast image out of *Spiritus Mundi*
Troubles my sight: somewhere in sands of the desert
A shape with lion body and the head of a man,
A gaze blank and pitiless as the sun,
Is moving its slow thighs, while all about it
Reel shadows of the indignant desert birds.
The darkness drops again; but now I know
That twenty centuries of stony sleep
Were vexed to nightmare by a rocking cradle,
And what rough beast, its hour come round at last,
Slouches towards Bethlehem to be born?

Observations

Famously written at the end of World War I, where millions died senselessly, and in the midst of a flu epidemic killing millions more, "The Second Coming" by William Butler Yeats is as bleak a poem as was ever written. Its topic is the dissolution of the world. Its language is mystical, its imagery violent and disturbing. The combination strikes us on a subconscious level and strikes hard. It makes us uncomfortable, unnerved. And yet, we can't look away.

Since its first publication, we've been drawn to "The Second Coming" again and again. It's one of the most anthologized poems of all time and has been quoted by seemingly everyone, in every media. Joan Didion. Oliver Stone. Stephen King. Lou Reed. Terry Pratchett and Neil Gaiman. It makes an appearance in not one but two episodes of *The Sopranos*. (I even included it in an episode of *Z Nation*.)

"The Second Coming" is iconic because it embodies, for better or worse, a timeless feeling. In 1920 it reflected the impact of war and disease on humanity. Today it could do the same. And telling us more about ourselves than perhaps we might like, its message is a terrible one. The second coming is at hand. But not the one that will reward the faithful. Instead, a perversion of that promise. The birthplace of Christ is now to be the birthplace of the "rough beast" that will bring the apocalypse. Terrifying. And, still, we can't look away.

About Craig Engler

Craig Engler is a writer and film producer and the former head of AMC Network's streaming horror service Shudder. He created the TV show *Z Nation*, which ran for five seasons on Syfy, and was executive producer of the spin-off series *Black Summer* on Netflix.

"Laughter's Dark Side"
by Travis Adams
A Brief Essay

Why is it that many resort to the darker side of humor when struggling with intense feelings of grief and loss, terminal diagnoses, and for some their daily work activities, specifically those in high-stress professions such as medical personnel, law enforcement, first responders, military, and mental health providers? How can someone find humor in dark and what may feel like hopeless times?

Many of us have heard that "laugher is the best medicine," and the reality is that sometimes even the darkest joke can bring light, laughter, and even amusement to a dire situation you may be facing. The term "gallows humor" or "black humor" is when a joke is made to help make a terrifying, life-threatening, serious, or painful experience more light-hearted and to break the tension and seriousness of the situation. Through humor, and specifically dark humor, professionals who are exposed to trauma, be it personally experienced or shared through discussion in detail, can find a way to see the next client, respond to the next incident, or prepare for the next emergency around the corner. By bringing humor into their lives, they can shake off the last trauma and bring a smile to the next. Laughter allows us to move through the tears, to push through pain, and often find acceptance in the situation we find ourselves in.

In a study conducted of social workers, half those questioned admitted to using gallows humor to help cope with their professional lives, many noting that it was a vital mechanism to release stress in connection to their work. Utilizing dark humor has been shown to aid in lowering physiological stress, reducing negative emotions, and lessening emotional distress when used with the right crowd. Typically, these comments are made between colleagues and coworkers and not to the general public; when working in many of these professions. Through gallows humor they find connection, levity, and comfort. Identifying and determining those who would understand and relate to gallows humor is important to not alienate oneself; remember, audience identification is important. If you find yourself laughing at an inappropriate time from some dark humor joke, just know that it is okay and it can, in fact, be very healthy and cathartic to move through pain, loss, and stress.

About Travis Adams

Travis Adams, LSW, clinical Counselor and Marine Corps veteran who specializes in working with service members struggling with their own mental health struggles after serving in the US Military. He combines mental health recovery with pop culture to make material understandable and relatable.

"The Shadow on the Stone"
by Thomas Hardy
Selected and with Commentary
by Ray Porter

I went by the Druid stone
That broods in the garden white and lone,
And I stopped and looked at the shifting shadows
That at some moments fall thereon
From the tree hard by with a rhythmic swing,
And they shaped in my imagining
To the shade that a well-known head and shoulders
Threw there when she was gardening.

I thought her behind my back,
Yea, her I long had learned to lack,
And I said: 'I am sure you are standing behind me,
Though how do you get into this old track?'
And there was no sound but the fall of a leaf
As a sad response; and to keep down grief
I would not turn my head to discover
That there was nothing in my belief.

Yet I wanted to look and see
That nobody stood at the back of me;
But I thought once more: 'Nay, I'll not unvision
A shape which, somehow, there may be.'
So I went on softly from the glade,
And left her behind me throwing her shade,
As she were indeed an apparition—
My head unturned lest my dream should fade.

Observations

If you've ever spent some time among standing stones in the UK (and a glance at my muddy boots over by the door will tell you I have), you will find a variety of people walking about them with crystals or incantations or an interpretation of an ancient ritual or (my favorite) a ritual of their own making.

I'm not talking about Stonehenge. That place is visually incredible but on another level it's a dead battery. No, you gotta walk. Get your boots out.

But when you get there, the stones seem to tell people a lot of things. What I'm told is that I'll never really know why they are there. Also, that I'm pretty much ephemeral. I can ascribe huge meaning or none and the stones don't mind. Whatever I feel or think (or say, if no one else is around), the stones don't mind. And it's okay with them.

And so, I impose myself on this poem. To me, it feels so terribly human. Am I haunted? Do I wish I was?

There's such grief here. But it's matter of fact. Not violins and tears. Mundane grief is infinitely more terrible to me than keening and wailing. It is vital, a part of life. The loneliness of it is stark and yet it's so beautiful to me. Or not. The stones don't mind either way.

About Ray Porter

Ray Porter is a Shakespearean actor and award-winning audiobook narrator. His reading of Andy Weir's *Project Hail Mary* was the 2021 Audiobook of the Year. He has worked on many titles by Jonathan Maberry, Scott Sigler, Dennis E. Taylor, Jack Carr, David Farland, Peter Clines, and many others. He has appeared in numerous movies and TV shows, including *Argo, Sons of Anarchy, Justified, Modern Family, Zack Snyder's Justice League, Will & Grace, It's Always Sunny in Philadelphia, Rebel Moon, Almost Famous, Monk*, and many others. When he's not exploring writing, he can be found either looking for ancient places in the UK or driving his child to hockey practice.

"THE SHIPWRECKED SAILOR" BY AMENI-AMENAA

SELECTED AND WITH COMMENTARY BY DAVID WELLINGTON

A Prose Poem
(an excerpt of a longer work)

A wave threw me on an island, after that I had been three days alone, without a companion beside my own heart. I laid me in a thicket, and the shadow covered me. Then stretched I my limbs to try to find something for my mouth. I found there figs and grain, melons of all kinds, fishes, and birds. Nothing was lacking. And I satisfied myself; and left on the ground that which was over, of what my arms had been filled withal. I dug a pit, I lighted a fire, and I made a burnt offering unto the gods.

Suddenly I heard a noise as of thunder, which I thought to be that of a wave of the sea. The trees shook, and the earth was moved. I uncovered my face, and I saw that a serpent drew near. He was thirty cubits long, and his beard greater than two cubits; his body was as overlaid with gold, and his color as that of true lazuli. He coiled himself before me. Then he opened his mouth, while that I lay on my face before him, and he said to me, "What has brought you, what has brought you, little one, what has brought you? If you say not speedily what has brought you to this isle, I will make you know yourself; as a flame you shall vanish, if you tell me not something I have not heard, or which I knew not, before you."

Then he took me in his mouth and carried me to his resting-place, and laid me down without any hurt. I was whole and sound, and nothing was gone from me. Then he opened his mouth against me, while that I lay on my face before him, and he said, "What has brought you, what has brought you, little one, what has brought you to this isle which is in the sea, and of which the shores are in the midst of the waves?'

Then I replied to him, and holding my arms low before him, I said to him, "I was embarked for the mines by the order of the majesty, in a ship, one hundred and fifty cubits was its length, and the width of it forty cubits. It had one hundred and fifty sailors of the best of Egypt, who had seen heaven and earth, and the hearts of whom were stronger than lions. They said that the wind would not be contrary, or that there would be none. Each of them exceeded his companion in the prudence of his heart and the strength of his arm, and I was not beneath any of them. A storm came upon us while we were on the sea. Hardly could we reach to the shore when the wind waxed yet greater, and the waves rose even eight cubits. As for me, I seized a piece of wood, while those who were in the boat perished without one being left with me for three days. Behold me now before you, for I was brought to this isle by a wave of the sea."

Then said he to me, "Fear not, fear not, little one, and make not your face sad. If you have come to me, it is God who has let you live. For it is He who has brought you to this isle of the blest, where nothing is lacking, and which is filled with all good things. See now, you shall pass one month after another, until you shall be four months in this isle. Then a ship shall come from your land with sailors, and you shall leave with them and go to your country, and you shall die in your town.

"Converse is pleasing, and he who tastes of it passes over his misery. I will therefore tell you of that which is in this isle. I am here with my brethren and my children around me; we are seventy-five serpents, children, and kindred; without naming a young girl who was brought unto me by chance, and on whom the fire of heaven fell, and burned her to ashes. As for you, if you are strong, and if your heart waits patiently, you shall press your infants to your bosom and embrace your wife. You shall return to your house which is full of all good things, you shall see your land, where you shall dwell in the midst of your kindred."

Observations

"The Shipwrecked Sailor" dates to 2200 BCE and is the oldest poem we know of, predating *The Epic of Gilgamesh* by two hundred years. It's a tale of adventure, survival, and a fantastical monster. And this is definitely a monster: the serpent in the story is enormous, powerful, threatening. It is in possession of both human and animal characteristics—a massive limbless body but also an impressive beard (two cubits long!) and the power of speech. It is also described as being like a manufactured object, its flesh compared to gold and lapis lazuli. It's a compelling creature design even today, and it isn't difficult to imagine the sailor's terror when the serpent appears in such a desolate location. Immediately it threatens to destroy the sailor, and he is helpless as it carries him away in its fang-filled mouth. Yet in the end, the serpent turns out to be friendly, as long as the sailor agrees to speak honestly and tell his tale. I find hints of Frankenstein's creature here, a combination of sublime power and heartbreaking loneliness. The serpent has lost its entire family, and also the companionship of a girl who seems to have been struck by lightning. No wonder it is glad to find another castaway, even if it knows (through magical powers of foresight) that the sailor's arrival heralds its own undoing. Once the sailor leaves the island the serpent knows its life will end as the island will sink into the waves. Eschewing flattery and lies, it seeks only conversation, and rewards the sailor greatly for this final gift of companionship.

It's not surprising that such an early work features a monster. We know that as long as humans have been making art, monsters have enthralled audiences. If this is the earliest known poem, the earliest known piece of sculpture is the Löwenmensch figure, a statuette of a human with the head of a lion or perhaps a bear. Carved from mammoth tusk forty thousand years ago, it still speaks to our fascination with the fearful, the savagely powerful creature that is both part of the natural world and yet simultaneously unreal, supranatural. One imagines that even further back, when our ancestors gathered around the first campfires, they must have told stories of what weird things prowled the darkness. In this sense, the shipwrecked sailor's giant serpent is merely one point in a long line that stretches throughout human culture, pointing toward the horror novels, films, and video games of the twenty-first century.

One final note: "The Shipwrecked Sailor" is not only the earliest poem but also the earliest work with an attributed author. The final lines of the poem (not included in the excerpt here) read, "This is finished from its beginning unto its end, even as it was found in a writing. It is written by the scribe of cunning fingers, Ameni-amenaa; may he live in life, wealth, and health!" Although it's possible Ameni-amenaa simply copied the story from an earlier source, I like to believe that he wrote this story and included his byline intentionally. As authors we often toil in obscurity, fearful of our limited posterity. It's nice to know that one writer's fingers, at least, can be remembered even four thousand years later!

About David Wellington

David Wellington is the author of over twenty novels of horror, suspense, and science fiction. He got his start serializing his novel *Monster Island* online in 2003. His most recent work includes *The Last Astronaut* and *Paradise-1*. He lives and works in New York City.

"The Sleeper"
by Edgar Allan Poe
Selected and with Commentary
by Joe R. Lansdale

At midnight, in the month of June,
I stand beneath the mystic moon.
An opiate vapor, dewy, dim,
Exhales from out her golden rim,
And softly dripping, drop by drop,
Upon the quiet mountain top,
Steals drowsily and musically
Into the universal valley.
The rosemary nods upon the grave;
The lily lolls upon the wave;
Wrapping the fog about its breast,
The ruin moulders into rest;
Looking like Lethe, see! the lake
A conscious slumber seems to take,
And would not, for the world, awake.
All Beauty sleeps!—and lo! where lies
Irene, with her Destinies!

Oh, lady bright! can it be right—
This window open to the night?
The wanton airs, from the tree-top,
Laughingly through the lattice drop—
The bodiless airs, a wizard rout,
Flit through thy chamber in and out,
And wave the curtain canopy
So fitfully—so fearfully—
Above the closed and fringéd lid
'Neath which thy slumb'ring soul lies hid,

That, o'er the floor and down the wall,
Like ghosts the shadows rise and fall!
Oh, lady dear, hast thou no fear?
Why and what art thou dreaming here?
Sure thou art come o'er far-off seas,
A wonder to these garden trees!
Strange is thy pallor! strange thy dress!
Strange, above all, thy length of tress,
And this all solemn silentness!

The lady sleeps! Oh, may her sleep,
Which is enduring, so be deep!
Heaven have her in its sacred keep!
This chamber changed for one more holy,
This bed for one more melancholy,
I pray to God that she may lie
Forever with unopened eye,
While the pale sheeted ghosts go by!

My love, she sleeps! Oh, may her sleep,
As it is lasting, so be deep!
Soft may the worms about her creep!
Far in the forest, dim and old,
For her may some tall vault unfold—
Some vault that oft hath flung its black
And wingéd pannels fluttering back,
Triumphant, o'er the crested palls
Of her grand family funerals—
Some sepulchre, remote, alone,
Against whose portals she hath thrown,
In childhood, many an idle stone—
Some tomb from out whose sounding door
She ne'er shall force an echo more,
Thrilling to think, poor child of sin!
It was the dead who groaned within.

Observations

In "The Sleeper" there is mention of a stone being thrown against a tomb's door, and how it must have made the dead inside groan. That imagery has haunted me for years.

To say the poem is dreamlike is an understatement, and though it deals with the idea of love eternal, it always made my skin crawl in a delicious way.

Like a cool breeze through an open window in the dead of night, ruffling the curtains, floating the smell of rotting dead flowers into a shadowed bedroom.

While reading the poem the imagination slithers like a snake. And to me its impact is better left visceral without evisceration of its delicate innards, which just might cause it to die on the academic autopsy table. It feels more than it explains, and that's as it should be.

About Joe R. Lansdale

Joe R. Lansdale is the author of fifty novels and four hundred shorter works, including stories, essays, reviews, film and TV scripts, stage plays, introductions, and magazine articles, as well as a book of poetry. His work has been made into films, animation, comics, and he has won numerous awards including the Edgar, the Raymond Chandler Lifetime Award, numerous Bram Stoker Awards, Lifetime Horror Award, and the Spur Award. He lives in Nacogdoches, Texas, with his wife, Karen, and pit bull, Rudy.

"The Spider and the Fly"
by Mary Howitt
Selected and with Commentary
by Scott Sigler

"Will you walk into my parlour?" said the Spider to the Fly,
"'Tis the prettiest little parlour that ever you did spy;
The way into my parlour is up a winding stair,
And I have many curious things to shew when you are
    there."
"Oh no, no," said the little Fly, "to ask me is in vain,
For who goes up your winding stair can ne'er come down
    again."

"I'm sure you must be weary, dear, with soaring up so high;
Will you rest upon my little bed?" said the Spider to the Fly.
"There are pretty curtains drawn around; the sheets are fine
    and thin,
And if you like to rest awhile, I'll snugly tuck you in!"
"Oh no, no," said the little Fly, "for I've often heard it said,
They never, never wake again, who sleep upon your bed!"

Said the cunning Spider to the Fly, "Dear friend what can
    I do,
To prove the warm affection I've always felt for you?
I have within my pantry, good store of all that's nice;
I'm sure you're very welcome—will you please to take a
    slice?"
"Oh no, no," said the little Fly, "kind Sir, that cannot be,
I've heard what's in your pantry, and I do not wish to see!"

"Sweet creature!" said the Spider, "you're witty and you're
    wise,

How handsome are your gauzy wings, how brilliant are
    your eyes!
I've a little looking-glass upon my parlour shelf,
If you'll step in one moment, dear, you shall behold
    yourself."
"I thank you, gentle Sir," she said, "for what you're pleased
    to say,
And bidding you good morning now, I'll call another day."

The Spider turned him round about, and went into his den,
For well he knew the silly Fly would soon come back again:
So he wove a subtle web, in a little corner sly,
And set his table ready, to dine upon the Fly.
Then he came out to his door again, and merrily did sing,
"Come hither, hither, pretty Fly, with the pearl and silver
    wing;
Your robes are green and purple—there's a crest upon your
    head;
Your eyes are like the diamond bright, but mine are dull as
    lead!"

Alas, alas! how very soon this silly little Fly,
Hearing his wily, flattering words, came slowly flitting by;
With buzzing wings she hung aloft, then near and nearer
    drew,
Thinking only of her brilliant eyes, and green and purple
    hue—
Thinking only of her crested head—poor foolish thing! At
    last,

Up jumped the cunning Spider, and fiercely held her fast.
He dragged her up his winding stair, into his dismal den,
Within his little parlour—but she ne'er came out again!
And now dear little children, who may this story read,
To idle, silly flattering words, I pray you ne'er give heed:
Unto an evil counsellor, close heart and ear and eye,
And take a lesson from this tale, of the Spider and the Fly.

While many dark poets resonate far more in the public conscience than Mary Howitt, few works created by those poets have had been so oft-quoted in other works than her tale "The Spider and the Fly."

Written in 1829, this warning about succumbing to empty flattery has a line that has transcended the poem itself and become a colloquialism, one that has endured for over almost two centuries. You know the line's cautionary intent as soon as you hear the words "said the spider to the fly."

That phrase, and variations/paraphrases of it, has woven its way into films and TV shows (such as *The Black Hole*, *Psycho*, *Teen Wolf*, *Archer*, the original *Batman* TV series, *Manifest*, *Sliders*), into songs by diverse artists (such as the Cure, Method Man, the Rolling Stones, Monster Magnet, Michael Franti & Spearhead, Venom, and Belle & Sebastian), and into more short stories and novels than one could likely count.

The spider got the fly, but Howitt's words got eternal life. Sometimes, sacrifices must be made.

About Scott Sigler

#1 *New York Times* bestselling author Scott Sigler is the creator of nineteen novels, seven novellas, and dozens of short stories. Scott is an inaugural inductee of the Podcasting Hall of Fame. Launched in 2005, *Scott Sigler Slices* is the world's longest-running fiction podcast. His loyal fans, who dubbed themselves "Sigler Junkies," have downloaded over fifty million episodes of Scott's work. Subscribe to the podcast at scottsigler.com/subscribe.

"The Twa Corbies"
by Author Unknown
Selected and with Commentary
by Seanan McGuire

As I was walking all alane,
I heard twa corbies making a mane;
The tane unto the t'other say,
'Where sall we gang and dine to-day?'

'In behint yon auld fail dyke,
I wot there lies a new-slain knight;
And naebody kens that he lies there,
But his hawk, his hound, and lady fair.

'His hound is to the hunting gane,
His hawk to fetch the wild-fowl hame,
His lady's ta'en another mate,
So we may mak our dinner sweet.

'Ye'll sit on his white hause-bane,
And I'll pike out his bonny blue een.
Wi' ae lock o' his gowden hair,
We'll theek our nest when it grows bare.

'Mony a ane for him makes mane,
But nane sall ken whare he is gane:
O'er his white banes, when they are bare,
The wind sall blaw for evermair.'

Observations

Written in a traditional Scots dialect, "The Twa Corbies" is often considered a variant of "The Three Ravens," which was originally collected in Childe's Ballads in 1611. This variant was originally published in 1803 and is still recorded and performed even into the present day.

The appeal of the poem is easy to see: the conversation between the two ravens is relatable and alien at the same time. This is not a discussion two humans might have about a human corpse, but it *is* a conversation two vulture-culture enthusiasts might have about a piece of roadkill! It casts the consequences of war into a tragic but entirely natural light. Of course, people die. Of course, ravens recycle them when that happens. Of course, the world goes on.

"The Twa Corbies" can sound strange to the American ear, given its Scots phrasing, cadence, and vocabulary, but it's a timeless narrative of loss and restoration, of finding something in what's been discarded. It was the first lullaby I can remember hearing, and I honestly think it's going to endure for another four hundred years, if not far longer.

About Seanan McGuire

Seanan McGuire is a writer of prose, comic books, and far too much poetry, and went to UC Berkeley for a folklore degree, which very much informs her taste in ballads.

"The Witch"
by Mary Elizabeth Coleridge
Selected and with Commentary
by Rio Youers

I have walked a great while over the snow,
And I am not tall nor strong.
My clothes are wet, and my teeth are set,
And the way was hard and long.

I have wandered over the fruitful earth,
But I never came here before.
Oh, lift me over the threshold, and let me in at the door!
The cutting wind is a cruel foe.

I dare not stand in the blast.
My hands are stone, and my voice a groan,
And the worst of death is past.
I am but a little maiden still,

My little white feet are sore.
Oh, lift me over the threshold, and let me in at the door!
Her voice was the voice that women have,
Who plead for their heart's desire.

She came—she came—and the quivering flame
Sunk and died in the fire.
It never was lit again on my hearth
Since I hurried across the floor,
To lift her over the threshold, and let her in at the door.

Observations

There's so much to unpack in this short, Victorian-era poem by Mary Elizabeth Coleridge. We have three stanzas, each subtly eerie, and each—as with all good poetry, and indeed art—open to interpretation. Who is this seemingly harmless "little maiden" who has wandered over the fruitful earth? And how has she endured such a "hard and long" journey?

I have read analyses that interpret the poem as an allegory of marriage, due principally to the final line of all three stanzas—the marital tradition of carrying the bride over the threshold. I would counter that the title suggests otherwise, and immediately engenders images of darkness and peril. Other interpretations suggest that "The Witch" touches on our fear of concealed evil (a false prophet—or wolf—in sheep's clothing, to borrow from the New Testament), as well as an inherent instinct to mistrust those things that appear too good to be true.

The concepts of trust, temptation, and deceit are touchpaper for all artists. They are prevalent in almost everything we choose to entertain ourselves with, from classic literature to reality TV shows. "The Witch" is a perfectly distilled example; it could be *Dracula* or *Fatal Attraction* in microcosm. I will also draw attention to the third stanza, where we see a seamless yet dramatic POV shift (something we are encouraged *not* to do in fiction, to avoid confounding the reader). Here we learn the outcome of the little maiden's visit: the quivering flame sinking and dying in the fire, never to be rekindled again. In other words: unending darkness and despair.

With a poem called "The Witch," I suppose it was too much to hope for a happy ending.

About Rio Youers

Rio Youers is the British Fantasy and Sunburst Award-nominated author of *Lola on Fire* and *No Second Chances*. His 2017 thriller *The Forgotten Girl* was a finalist for the Arthur Ellis Award for Best Crime Novel. He is the writer of *Refrigerator Full of Heads*, a six-issue comic series from DC Comics, and *Sleeping Beauties*, a graphic novel based on the number-one bestseller by Stephen King and Owen King. Rio's latest novel, *The Bang-Bang Sisters*, was published by William Morrow in summer 2024.

"The Witches Spell"
by William Shakespeare
Selected and with Commentary by Simon Vance

(Macbeth, Act IV, Scene 1)

First Witch
Thrice the brinded cat hath mewed.

Second Witch
Thrice, and once the hedge-pig whined.

Third Witch
Harpier cries, "'Tis time, 'tis time!"

First Witch
Round about the cauldron go;
In the poisoned entrails throw.
Toad, that under cold stone
Days and nights has thirty-one
Sweltered venom, sleeping got,
Boil thou first i' th' charmèd pot.

All
Double, double toil and trouble;
Fire burn, and cauldron bubble.

Second Witch
Fillet of a fenny snake
In the cauldron boil and bake.
Eye of newt and toe of frog,
Wool of bat and tongue of dog,

Adder's fork and blindworm's sting,
Lizard's leg and howlet's wing,
For a charm of powerful trouble,
Like a hell-broth boil and bubble.

All
Double, double toil and trouble;
Fire burn, and cauldron bubble.

Third Witch
Scale of dragon, tooth of wolf,
Witches' mummy, maw and gulf
Of the ravined salt-sea shark,
Root of hemlock digged i' th' dark,
Liver of blaspheming Jew,
Gall of goat, and slips of yew
Slivered in the moon's eclipse,
Nose of Turk and Tartar's lips,
Finger of birth-strangled babe
Ditch-delivered by a drab,
Make the gruel thick and slab.
Add thereto a tiger's chaudron
For th' ingredients of our cauldron.

All
Double, double, toil and trouble;
Fire burn, and cauldron bubble.

Second Witch
Cool it with a baboon's blood.
Then the charm is firm and good.
[Enter Hecate, goddess of witchcraft]

Hecate
O, well done! I commend your pains,
And everyone shall share i' th' gains.
And now about the cauldron sing
Like elves and fairies in a ring,
Enchanting all that you put in.

Second Witch
By the pricking of my thumbs,
Something wicked this way comes.
Open, locks,
Whoever knocks.

Observations

Welcome to the Great British Baking Show of 1606. Your challenge for this round ...

Horror for me is all about the "feels" and every line of the witches' spell brings a different picture to mind—more than twenty ingredients, each of which, if you visualize them, is enough to make you squirm. Altogether not a soup I'd like to taste.

Where did Shakespeare source all these ingredients for the weird (or wayward) sisters' spell? I've seen it suggested it was based on an actual occult spell (and thus the reason his "Scottish Play" is so ... unlucky) or, at the more mundane end of the spectrum, that many of the items are just country names for rather ordinary things ("Eye of Newt" being another name for mustard seed). But that would be disappointing.

Maybe there's a hidden message? Years ago, in Burl Ives's suite in the Brighton Grand Hotel, I was introduced to a professor who claimed that Shakespeare (if it was indeed he who wrote the plays!) had placed ciphers in his texts that, once broken, pointed to the location of hidden bunkers of treasure in New England.

Yeah ... or maybe not.

As in the postscript to many horror tales: Perhaps we'll never know the truth.

Personally, I like to think that John Lennon in writing "yellow matter custard, dripping from a dead dog's eye" in "I Am the Walrus" had a rare Shakespearean-inspired moment ... or if you believe that time is a flat circle, maybe Shakespeare had a rare Lennon moment.

Now wouldn't that be wyrd?

About Simon Vance

Simon Vance is an audiobook narrator and actor who performs contemporary literary works as well as classics, children's books, and nonfiction. He has narrated over one thousand audiobooks and won sixteen Audie Awards since 2002. Specializing in single-voice narration, he was named the American Library Association's Booklist Magazine Voice of Choice in 2008 and has earned AudioFile Magazine's Earphones Award for more than sixtyperformances since 1998. He has also narrated audiobooks under the names of Richard Matthews and Robert Whitfield. He lives in Los Angeles, California.

"THE YUKI-ONNA"
BY LAFCADIO HEARN
SELECTED AND WITH COMMENTARY
BY KEVIN WETMORE

Yuki-Onna—
Yosō kushi mo
Atsu kōri;
Sasu-kōgai ya
Kōri naruran.
[As for the Snow-Woman,—even her best comb, if I mistake not, is made of thick ice; and her hair-pin, too, is probably made of ice.]
Honrai wa
Kū naru mono ka,
Yuki-Onna?
Yoku-yoku mireba
Ichi-butsu mo nashi!
[Was she, then, a delusion from the very first, that Snow-Woman,—a thing that vanishes into empty space? When I look carefully all about me, not one trace of her is to be seen!]
Yo-akéréba
Kiété yuku é wa
Shirayuki no
Onna to mishi mo
Yanagi nari-keri!
[Having vanished at daybreak (that Snow-Woman), none could say whither she had gone. But what had seemed to be a snow-white woman became indeed a willow-tree!]
Yuki-Onna
Mité wa yasathiku,
Matsu wo ori
Nama-daké hishigu
Chikara ari-keri!

[Though the Snow-Woman appears to sight slender and gentle, yet, to snap the pine-trees asunder and to crush the live bamboos, she must have had strength.]
Samukésa ni
Zotto wa surédo
Yuki-Onna,—
Yuki oré no naki
Yanagi-goshi ka mo!
[Though the Snow-Woman makes one shiver by her coldness,—ah, the willowy grace of her form cannot be broken by the snow (i.e. she charms you despite the cold she embodies).]

Observations

Lafcadio Hearn is a fascinating cat—born in Greece in 1850 to a Greek mother and Irish father who died while he was still a child, he was raised by a great-aunt who wanted him to be a priest. Instead, he became a journalist and traveled the world, living in New Orleans, Cincinnati, the Caribbean, and New York before finally moving to Japan in 1890, where he married a Japanese woman, took the name Koizumi Yakumo, and wrote numerous books on Japanese culture and literature, the most famous of which are his tales of the supernatural, *In Ghostly Japan* and *Kwaidan*. The latter was a gathering of Japanese folktales of ghosts and monsters that inspired the 1964 Kobayashi Masaki film of the same name.

The *Yōka Hyaku-Monogatari* is a book of poetry taken from a collection of ghost stories rooted in a game samurai used to play called "Hyaku Monogatari," literally "one hundred stories." As the sun sets, a group of people light a hundred candles. They then tell short ghost stories or poems, and at the end of each story or poem, a candle is blown out. After one hundred stories and poems have been recited and the last candle blown out, any ghosts present will make themselves known. It's a fun game—you should try it. The Japanese original was collected by Jingorō Takumi who wrote under the nom de plume Temmér Réōjin. The poems were strings of *kyoka*—"mad poetry"—about different monsters and ghosts. Hearn edited the book down, selecting the poem series that he thought would be of interest and accessible to western readers.

The poem cycle here is the *kyoka* for the Yuki-Onna, the snow-woman, who in Japanese folklore is an embodiment of the cold and ice, whose embrace is death. One of the best-known stories from *Kwaidan* concerns a man who meets and later unknowingly marries a Yuki-Onna. The poems here (with Hearn's translations) tell of a man who scares himself by thinking he sees a Yuki-Onna coming for him at night, but the next morning realizes it was just a snow-covered willow tree.

About Kevin Wetmore

Kevin Wetmore is a professor of Theatre Arts at Loyola Marymount University, a writer, director, actor, and stage combat choreographer who is also a five-time Bram Stoker Award nominee. He is the author or editor of over thirty books, including *Post-9/11 Horror in American Cinema*, *Devil's Advocates: The Conjuring*, *Eaters of the Dead: Myths and Realities of Cannibal Monsters*, *Modern Asian Theatre and Performance 1900-2000*, *The Metheun Anthology of Modern Asian Drama*, and *The Streaming of Hill House*. He has also written over a hundred book chapters and journal articles on everything from monster wars of civilization, Godzilla on stage, and theology and zombies, and has also published over three dozen short stories.

"They Flee from Me"
by Sir Thomas Wyatt

Selected and with Commentary
by Mary A. Turzillo

They flee from me that sometime did me seek
With naked foot, stalking in my chamber.
I have seen them gentle, tame, and meek,
That now are wild and do not remember
That sometime they put themself in danger
To take bread at my hand; and now they range,
Busily seeking with a continual change.

Thanked be fortune it hath been otherwise
Twenty times better; but once in special,
In thin array after a pleasant guise,
When her loose gown from her shoulders did fall,
And she me caught in her arms long and small;
Therewithal sweetly did me kiss
And softly said, "Dear heart, how like you this?"

It was no dream: I lay broad waking.
But all is turned thorough my gentleness
Into a strange fashion of forsaking;
And I have leave to go of her goodness,
And she also, to use newfangleness.
But since that I so kindly am served
I would fain know what she hath deserved.

Observations

I first became fascinated by this poem when I was in grad school. My department was a hotbed of clandestine love affairs and power battles—much like Henry VIII's court. I could not, and still cannot, get beyond a broad and patent interpretation of "They Flee from Me"—a plaint of a limerence experience I myself experienced: a suitor woos us with gifts, words, poetry, pursuit, embraces. Then when we succumb and fall in love with them, they suddenly reverse and reject us. This must have happened to Wyatt. I know there are mysteries about who "she" was (Anne Boleyn?), but it's clear to me that this is the stab-to-the-heart meaning of the poem. I was struck by the seemingly unfinished scansion of the last lines, but I've grown to love its awkwardness; it grindingly expresses Wyatt's agony and anger at the reversal.

About Mary A. Turzillo

Mary A. Turzillo is a fiction writer and poet, winner of a Nebula and one-and-a-half Elgins. Her latest books are *Cast from Darkness* (2023) with Marge Simon, and *Cosmic Cats and Fantastic Furballs* (2022).

"This Living Hand" by John Keats

Submitted and with Commentary by Marge Simon

This living hand, now warm and capable
Of earnest grasping, would, if it were cold
And in the icy silence of the tomb,
So haunt thy days and chill thy dreaming nights
That thou would wish thine own heart dry of blood
So in my veins red life might stream again,
And thou be conscience-calm'd—see here it is—
I hold it towards you.

Observations

With a minor in English Lit, and a particular interest in the Romantic era, I chose a poem by John Keats. Keats's contrasts grabbed me from the start (warm/cold, dry/stream) and, of course, the mention of blood. I immediately related it to a human speaking to a vampire in their coffin. Indeed, Keats could be referring to his own hand reaching to touch a lover, and alluding to his chances of an early death, due to tuberculosis. As poets may do when inspired by lines of another poet, I wrote my own version (shown here under the original), adding a note of scornful dismissal.

About Marge Simon

Marge Simon is a writer/poet/illustrator living in Ocala, FL, USA. A multiple Stoker winner, Horror Writers Association Lifetime Achievement awardee, and Grand Master of Science Fiction Poetry Association, her works appear in *Asimov's, Daily Science Fiction, JoCCA, Silver Blade, Magazine of Fantasy & Science Fiction*, and more, as well as anthologies such as *Weird Tales, Scary Out There, Chiral Mad, Qualia Nous, Birthing Monsters*, and *What Remains*, Firbolg Publishing. Instagram: margesimonwrites

"To——. Ulalume: A Ballad" by Edgar Allan Poe

Selected and with Commentary by Josh Malerman

The skies they were ashen and sober;
The leaves they were crispéd and sere—
The leaves they were withering and sere;
It was night in the lonesome October
Of my most immemorial year;
It was hard by the dim lake of Auber,
In the misty mid region of Weir—
It was down by the dank tarn of Auber,
In the ghoul-haunted woodland of Weir.

Here once, through an alley Titanic,
Of cypress, I roamed with my Soul—
Of cypress, with Psyche, my Soul.
These were days when my heart was volcanic
As the scoriac rivers that roll—
As the lavas that restlessly roll
Their sulphurous currents down Yaanek
In the ultimate climes of the pole—
That groan as they roll down Mount Yaanek
In the realms of the boreal pole.

Our talk had been serious and sober,
But our thoughts they were palsied and sere—
Our memories were treacherous and sere—
For we knew not the month was October,
And we marked not the night of the year—
(Ah, night of all nights in the year!)
We noted not the dim lake of Auber—

(Though once we had journeyed down here)—
We remembered not the dank tarn of Auber,
Nor the ghoul-haunted woodland of Weir.

And now, as the night was senescent
And star-dials pointed to morn—
As the star-dials hinted of morn—
At the end of our path a liquescent
And nebulous lustre was born,
Out of which a miraculous crescent
Arose with a duplicate horn.
Astarte's bediamonded crescent
Distinct with its duplicate horn.

And I said—"She is warmer than Dian:
She rolls through an ether of sighs—
She revels in a region of sighs:
She has seen that the tears are not dry on
These cheeks, where the worm never dies,
And has come past the stars of the Lion
To point us the path to the skies—
To the Lethean peace of the skies—
Come up, in despite of the Lion,
To shine on us with her bright eyes—
Come up through the lair of the Lion,
With love in her luminous eyes."

But Psyche, uplifting her finger,
Said—"Sadly this star I mistrust—
Her pallor I strangely mistrust:—
Oh, hasten! oh, let us not linger!
Oh, fly!—let us fly!—for we must."
In terror she spoke, letting sink her
Wings till they trailed in the dust—
In agony sobbed, letting sink her
Plumes till they trailed in the dust—
Till they sorrowfully trailed in the dust.

I replied—"This is nothing but dreaming:
Let us on by this tremulous light!
Let us bathe in this crystalline light!
Its Sybilic splendor is beaming
With Hope and in Beauty to-night:—
See!—it flickers up the sky through the night!
Ah, we safely may trust to its gleaming,

And be sure it will lead us aright—
We safely may trust to a gleaming
That cannot but guide us aright,
Since it flickers up to Heaven through the night."

Thus I pacified Psyche and kissed her,
And tempted her out of her gloom—
And conquered her scruples and gloom:
And we passed to the end of the vista,
But were stopped by the door of a tomb—
By the door of a legended tomb;
And I said—"What is written, sweet sister,
On the door of this legended tomb?"
She replied—"Ulalume—Ulalume—
'Tis the vault of thy lost Ulalume!"

Then my heart it grew ashen and sober
As the leaves that were crispèd and sere—
As the leaves that were withering and sere,
And I cried—"It was surely October
On *this* very night of last year
That I journeyed—I journeyed down here—
That I brought a dread burden down here—
On this night of all nights in the year,
Oh, what demon has tempted me here?
Well I know, now, this dim lake of Auber—
This misty mid region of Weir—
Well I know, now, this dank tarn of Auber—

In the ghoul-haunted woodland of Weir."
Said *we*, then—the two, then—"Ah, can it
Have been that the woodlandish ghouls—
The pitiful, the merciful ghouls—
To bar up our way and to ban it
From the secret that lies in these wolds—
From the thing that lies hidden in these wolds—
Had drawn up the spectre of a planet
From the limbo of lunary souls—
This sinfully scintillant planet
From the Hell of the planetary souls?"

Observations

Do you hear it? That's the musicality of the macabre. And I think it's the reason we all trust Edgar Allan Poe as much as we do. It's one thing to be interested in morbidities, and that's a fine interest (as we well know), but it's another to record the music they make in the prose and poetry you write. That's were Poe's slip is always showing (thank heavens); that's where we see the authenticity we're all (justifiably) suckers for, whether we declare this need in ourselves or not. Sometimes I read Poe just to point out to myself that seemingly every line he writes contains shadows and the music of those shadows, so that it's hard for me not to imagine him writing in a dimly lit room (or pub) as devils and ghouls pluck black violins and blow into bone white flutes.

Is it any wonder he was drawn to poetry, that poetry makes up half the output of his artistic life? The man unearthed the music of the damned, giving us works such as "Ulalume," in which our narrator walks sadly, without concrete aim, through "night in the lonesome October" (I know you hear the tones and trills in *that* line), conversing with his soul, only to discover he's walked directly to the tomb of his lost, his beloved deceased. Oh, how grueling. Because whether we've experienced this exact loss ourselves, we do know *loss*, and the knack it has of delivering us (repetitiously, often at key moments in the course of our life) back to that which we lost, whether we'd planned on visiting or not.

It's Poe's music. And we're dancing to it. Subconscious motivation is a thing unseen, invisible as ... music. And the narrator of "Ulalume" strikes a chord (born of cellos and bassoons, accompanied by deep drums) that moves us because it's in us, too, this inability (and perhaps a lack of desire; who wants to forget such things?) to recognize what might be on our own minds. Scary is a sound, but Gothic sorrow a song. The man wrote this poem in 1847. And what travels through time intact and untouched quite like true music?

About Josh Malerman

Josh Malerman is *The New York Times* bestselling author of *Bird Box* and *Incidents Around the House*. He's also one of two singer/songwriters for the Michigan rock band the High Strung, whose newest album *Address Unknown* was released just last year. He lives in Michigan with the artist/musician Allison Laakko and their many (wonderful) pets.

"Tomino's Hell" by Saijō Yaso
Selected and with Commentary by Jamie Ford

His younger sister spits out fire,
While sweet Tomino's soul expires.
Alone, he falls in hell's deep gloom,
Where not a single flower bloom.
Does his older sister wield the whip?
The crimson lash, his thoughts do grip.
Beating, striking, not quite breaking,
On hell's dark road, his soul is aching.
I pray for guidance, cast darkest spell,
To lead the boy from deepest hell.
Put all you can in leather sack,
This journey's long, no turning back.
Spring awakes in forest glades,
And in hell's deep valley darkness shades.
The nightingale in cage it sings
The sheep in cart, solace they bring.
Tears on the cheeks of sweet Tomino,
As he lives out this tale of woe.
Sing, nightingale, in rainy mist,
For little sister, whom he has missed.
His cry resounds through hell's domain,
As fox-peonies bloom in pain.
'round seven mountains, valleys deep,
Tomino's journey, he must keep.
If they too are here, let them be shown,
The mountain, needles, pins are sewn.
The pins don't pierce, but softly mark,
Tomino's path through endless dark.

OBSERVATIONS

According to legend, this poem was written by a Japanese boy named Tomino. Because of the gruesome nature of this piece, Tomino's parents punished him by locking him in their basement, where he fell ill and subsequently died.

Originally published in 1919, "Tomino's Hell" has taken on a life—or death—of its own and has become known as the "cursed poem" in that bad things befall those who read it out loud. Do you dare? (I didn't.)

ABOUT JAMIE FORD

Jamie Ford is the great-grandson of Nevada mining pioneer, Min Chung, who emigrated from Hoiping, China, to San Francisco in 1865, where he adopted the western name "Ford," thus confusing countless generations. His debut novel *Hotel on the Corner of Bitter and Sweet* spent two years on *The New York Times* bestseller list. His latest bestselling novel is *The Many Daughters of Afong Moy*.

"Waltzing Matilda"
by Andrew Barton
"Banjo" Paterson

Selected and with Commentary by Robbie Coburn

Tomorrow, the bandages
will come off. I wonder
will I see half an orange,
half an apple, half my
mother's face
with my one remaining eye?

I did not see the bullet
but felt its pain
exploding in my head.
His image did not
vanish, the soldier
with a big gun, unsteady
hands, and look in
his eyes
I could not understand

I can see him so clearly
with my eyes closed,
it could be that inside our heads
we each have one spare set
of eyes
to make up for the ones we lose

Next month, on my birthday,
I'll have a brand new glass eye,
maybe things will look round
and fat in the middle—

I've gazed through all my marbles,
they made the world look strange.

I hear a nine-month old
has also lost an eye,
I wonder if my soldier
shot her too—a soldier
looking for little girls who
look him in the eye—
I'm old enough, almost four,
I've seen enough of life,
but she's just a baby
who didn't know any better.

Observations

"Waltzing Matilda" (written in 1895, but not published until 1903) is an Australian bush ballad with lyrics penned by Banjo Paterson. It is widely considered to be Australia's unofficial national anthem. In Australian slang, "waltzing" refers to foot travel, and "matilda" is another term for a swag (a bedroll carried on one's back).

Most people in Australia and abroad, young and old, know the lyrics and tune to "Waltzing Matilda," but what fascinates me about this piece is that at its core, it is a ghost story. One that veils its meaning beneath its catchy, seemingly joyous refrain.

The narrative of the verse focuses on a swagman (an itinerant traveller) boiling a pot of tea (billy) at a bush camp "by a billabong" (small body of water). He then captures a sheep (jumbuck) who stops to drink from the water, with the intention of eating it. The owner of the sheep, accompanied by three policemen (troopers) comes after the swagman to arrest him for theft, but to evade punishment, he commits suicide by jumping into the billabong.

The swagman then haunts the place where he died, and "his ghost may be heard as you pass by that billabong."

As a child, my mother would read my brothers and me the verse of Banjo Paterson.

Growing up on a farm in Victoria with several dams located in vast paddocks, I could visualise the swagman waiting for his billy to boil and capturing the jumbuck, then jumping into the water to escape the troopers. At night, surrounded by gumtrees beneath the dark sky, I could imagine the ghost of the swagman haunting the space surrounding the water, an ominous, terrifying mist enveloping the paddock.

About Robbie Coburn

Robbie Coburn is an Australian poet based in Melbourne. Judith Beveridge wrote that his work "is so raw yet so luminous and piercing to the point where the poetry is utterly transformative." His books include *Ghost Poetry* (Upswell Publishing, 2024), *And I Could Not Have Hurt You* (Kiddiepunk, 2023), and *The Other Flesh* (UWA Publishing, 2019). His poems have been published in *Poetry*, *Meanjin*, *Island*, *Westerly*, and elsewhere, and anthologized in books including *Writing to the Wire* (UWA Publishing, 2016) and *To End All Wars* (Puncher & Wattmann, 2018). He began writing poetry at the age of fourteen, inspired by the works of Edgar Allan Poe.

"We Wear the Mask"
Paul Laurence Dunbar
Selected and with Commentary by Maurice Broaddus

We wear the mask that grins and lies,
It hides our cheeks and shades our eyes,—
This debt we pay to human guile;
With torn and bleeding hearts we smile,
And mouth with myriad subtleties.
Why should the world be over-wise,
In counting all our tears and sighs?
Nay, let them only see us, while
We wear the mask.
We smile, but, O great Christ, our cries
To thee from tortured souls arise.
We sing, but oh the clay is vile
Beneath our feet, and long the mile;
But let the world dream otherwise,
We wear the mask!

Observations

The poem was a reaction to the Black experience of living in America. Not too long after the Civil War ended, when life seemed to improve a bit only to have racism rear its head again, more vicious than ever. Dunbar compares living in the shadow of oppressive systems, laws, and culture to hiding one's suffering behind a joyful face. Our happiness is a lie. Sadly, not too much has changed.

This poem inspired one of my early novellas, *Devil's Marionette*. The story follows the life of Kevon "Ebony" Williamson, the Black star of an *In*

Living Color/*Saturday Night Live*-type sketch comedy show called *Chocolate City*. The set has been plagued by a series of mishaps culminating in the death of one of their co-stars. He and the show's creator, James Morris, try to hold the cast together (against each other as well as the network executives trying to exert their vision onto the show) in preparation for their live show. The set has come under siege by ghosts of their past. Each crew member has to wrestle with their own demons even as a terror wreaks havoc on their lives. The spirit of Bert Williams, a Black vaudeville clown minstrel who performed in blackface, haunts not only the set, but Kevon and one of his costars ... to tragic consequence. It's about how and what an artist is willing to compromise in order to have success.

Devil's Marionette was tough for me to write. I wrote it from a painful, angry place as I had been thinking about the struggle of Black artists against the pressures and expectations of the community, the failure to live up to that unspoken obligation, and the yoke of a history of racism. I wrestled with the role of the Black artist: his responsibility to his craft and to the community. The compromises we sometimes make as creatives in order to sell "to the market" reducing us to "still cooning for massa's amusement." I wanted to immerse the reader into the lives of the cast and crew so that they felt the oppressive weight of hundreds of years of hatred, supremacy, and racism. To have the pain hollow them out leaving them with only their dark night of the soul to find their way out of. They have to struggle with their own darkness.

About Maurice Broaddus

An award-winning Afrofuturist and librarian, he's had over a hundred short stories published in such places as *Lightspeed Magazine*, *Black Panther: Tales from Wakanda*, *Out There Screaming*, *Asimov's*, *Weird Tales*, *Magazine of Fantasy & Science Fiction*, and *Uncanny Magazine*. With over a dozen novels in print, his latest include *Sweep of Stars*, *Breath of Oblivion*, *Unfadeable*, *Pimp My Airship*, and *The Usual Suspects*. Learn more at MauriceBroaddus.com

"We Will All Go Together When We Go" by Tom Lehrer

Selected and with Commentary by Linda Nagle

When you attend a funeral,
It is sad to think that sooner o'
Later those you love will do the same for you.
And you may have thought it tragic,
Not to mention other adjec-
-Tives, to think of all the weeping they will do.
But don't you worry.
No more ashes, no more sackcloth,
And an armband made of black cloth
Will some day never more adorn a sleeve.
For if the bomb that drops on you.
Gets your friends and neighbors, too,
There'll be nobody left behind to grieve.
And we will all go together when we go.
What a comforting fact that is to know.
Universal bereavement,
An inspiring achievement,
Yes, we all will go together when we go.
We will all go together when we go.
All suffused with an incandescent glow.
No one will have the endurance
To collect on his insurance,
Lloyd's of London will be loaded when they go.
We will all fry together when we fry.
We'll be french fried potatoes by and by.
There will be no more misery
When the world is our rotizerie,
Yes, we will all fry together when we fry.

Down by the old maelstrom,
There'll be a storm before the calm.
And we will all bake together when we bake.
There'll be nobody present at the wake.
With complete participation
In that grand incineration,
Nearly three billion hunks of well-done steak.
Oh, we will all char together when we char.
And let there be no moaning of the bar.
Just sing out a Te Deum
When you see that I.C.B.M.,
And the party will be "come as you are."
Oh, we will all burn together when we burn.
There'll be no need to stand and wait your turn.
When it's time for the fallout
And Saint Peter calls us all out,
We'll just drop our agendas and adjourn.
You will all go directly to your respective
Valhallas.
Go directly, do not pass Go,
Do not collect two hundred dolla's.
We will all go together when we go.
Ev'ry Hottenhot and ev'ry Eskimo.
When the air becomes uranious,
We will all go simultaneous.
Yes, we all will go together
When we all go together,
Yes, we all will go together when we go.

OBSERVATIONS

Done well, political horror gives me the feels. When it's *Lehrer's* political horror, conveyed via haunting, devastating satire and achingly brilliant wordplay ... damn, bruh. I could live on this stuff. Breakfast, lunch, and dinner, and gratuitous snacks between meals. It's nothing short of poetic sustenance to literature lovers the world over; anathema to the compassionless. What better way to convey the horrors of war—and the anxieties it so often enables—than with a rousing chorus? "We Will All Go Together When We Go" is an altogether devastating piece masquerading as clever comedy: the effortless M.O. of the ultimate savant satirist. Bringing real-life horror right down to earth, landing each rhyme with a V2-*boom* is one of Tom Lehrer's (many) fortes, and this 'un gets me where I live.

"Just sing out a Te Deum / when you see that I.C.B.M." Did you see that sexy assonance walk by? That rhyme, man. It's a heartbeat. The whole thing is a portrait: can you, like me, see the fear on every atomic-age face? Do you smell the panic? But do you also sense the hope? That togetherness —whatever the catalyst—might ... *just might* be feasible?

Dark and thought-provoking, not unlike Lehrer himself, the lyrics reflect not only the unease of the Cold War era, but the timeless, harsh reality that we are all in this together, folks. War is indiscriminate. *Nuclear* war, even more so. And the resonance of the piece is only to be expected when one writes so enduringly.

About Linda Nagle

Linda is an author, poet, screenwriter and editor, whose stories can be found in a variety of anthologies, including *Great British Horror— Midsummer Eve* (Black Shuck Books) and the Shirley Jackson Award-nominated *Stitched Lips* (Dragon's Roost Press). In 2015, First Frame Films produced her first crime series, *tráfico*, whose lower-case "*t*" annoys the hell out of her. You may also find her on social media at any given moment, being that she doesn't sleep. Oh, and she blogs (what's left of) her brain out here: liberatetutemet.com

"What the Moon Brings"
by H.P. Lovecraft
Selected and with Commentary by Maxwell I. Gold

A Prose Poem

I hate the moon—I am afraid of it—for when it shines on certain scenes familiar and loved it sometimes makes them unfamiliar and hideous.

It was in the spectral summer when the moon shone down on the old garden where I wandered; the spectral summer of narcotic flowers and humid seas of foliage that bring wild and many-colouredured dreams. And as I walked by the shallow crystal stream I saw unwonted ripples tipped with yellow light, as if those placid waters were drawn on in resistless currents to strange oceans that are not in the world. Silent and sparkling, bright and baleful, those moon-cursed waters hurried I knew not whither; whilst from the embowered banks white lotos blossoms fluttered one by one in the opiate night-wind and dropped despairingly into the stream, swirling away horribly under the arched, carven bridge, and staring back with the sinister resignation of calm, dead faces.

And as I ran along the shore, crushing sleeping flowers with heedless feet and maddened ever by the fear of unknown things and the lure of the dead faces, I saw that the garden had no end under that moon; for where by day the walls were, there stretched now only new vistas of trees and paths, flowers and shrubs, stone idols and pagodas, and bendings of the yellow-litten stream past grassy banks and under grotesque bridges of marble. And the lips of the dead lotos-faces whispered sadly, and bade me follow, nor did I cease my steps till the stream became a river, and joined amidst marshes of swaying reeds and beaches of gleaming sand the shore of a vast and nameless sea.

Upon that sea the hateful moon shone, and over its unvocal waves weird perfumes brooded. And as I saw therein the lotos-faces vanish, I longed for nets that I might capture them and learn from them the secrets which the moon had brought upon the night. But when the moon went over to the west and the still tide ebbed from the sullen shore, I saw in that light old spires that the waves almost uncovered, and white columns gay with festoons of green seaweed. And knowing that to this sunken place all the dead had come, I trembled and did not wish again to speak with the lotos-faces.

Yet when I saw afar out in the sea a black condor descend from the sky to seek rest on a vast reef, I would fain have questioned him, and asked him of those whom I had known when they were alive. This I would have asked him had he not been so far away, but he was very far, and could not be seen at all when he drew nigh that gigantic reef.

So I watched the tide go out under that sinking moon, and saw gleaming the spires, the towers, and the roofs of that dead, dripping city. And as I watched, my nostrils tried to close against the perfume-conquering stench of the world's dead; for truly, in this unplaced and forgotten spot had all the flesh of the churchyards gathered for puffy sea-worms to gnaw and glut upon.

Over those horrors the evil moon now hung very low, but the puffy worms of the sea need no moon to feed by. And as I watched the ripples that told of the writhing of worms beneath, I felt a new chill from afar out whither the condor had flown, as if my flesh had caught a horror before my eyes had seen it.

Nor had my flesh trembled without cause, for when I raised my eyes I saw that the waters had ebbed very low, shewing much of the vast reef whose rim I had seen before. And when I saw that this reef was but the black basalt crown of a shocking eikon whose monstrous forehead now shone in the dim moonlight and whose vile hooves must paw the hellish ooze miles below, I shrieked and shrieked lest the hidden face rise above the waters, and lest the hidden eyes look at me after the slinking away of that leering and treacherous yellow moon.

And to escape this relentless thing I plunged gladly and unhesitatingly into the stinking shallows where amidst weedy walls and sunken streets fat sea-worms feast upon the world's dead.

Observations

"I hate the moon," remarks the opening line of H.P. Lovecraft's prose poem "What the Moon Brings," originally published May 5th, 1923, in the *National Amateur*. Often considered a short story, this piece actually falls into the category of Lovecraft's few prose poems—"Nyarlathotep" (1920), "Ex Oblivione" (1921), "Nemesis" (1918)—and though Lovecraft was known mainly for his prose, according to weird fiction scholar S.T. Joshi, "this is because he never truly found a distinctive voice as a poet."

Though this poem is a poignant and visceral smack in the face by the narrator, utilizing Lovecraft's distinctive prose coupled by a strong sense of dread and uncertainty. The narrator is trapped between the crushing weight of madness, or welcoming death gladly. The poem takes the reader on a wild, dark journey through the deranged dreamscape, until we are left not knowing whether the narrator has accepted his fate, is lost to wander the bizarre garden beneath the guise of the moon, or chose death.

While Lovecraft may not be remembered by most as a poet, his conceptions and poetic precision will continue to intrigue and beguile us when we look up towards that pallid object in the sky. Perhaps we, too, we may hate the moon.

About Maxwell I. Gold

Maxwell I. Gold is an acclaimed Jewish American cosmic horror poet and editor with an extensive body of work comprising over three hundred poems since 2017. His writings have earned a place alongside many literary luminaries in the speculative fiction genre. His work has appeared in numerous literary journals, magazines, and anthologies such as *Weird Tales Magazine*, *Startling Stories*, *Space and Time Magazine*, *Other Terrors: An Inclusive Anthology*, *Chiral Mad 5*, and many more. Maxwell's work has been recognized with multiple nominations including the Rhysling Award, the Pushcart Prize, and the Bram Stoker Awards. Find him and his work at thewellsoftheweird.com.

"The Stolen Child"
by William Butler Yeats
Selected and with Commentary by Jonathan Maberry

Where dips the rocky highland
Of Sleuth Wood in the lake,
There lies a leafy island
Where flapping herons wake
The drowsy water rats;
There we've hid our faery vats,
Full of berrys
And of reddest stolen cherries.
Come away, O human child!
To the waters and the wild
With a faery, hand in hand,
For the world's more full of weeping than you can understand.
Where the wave of moonlight glosses
The dim gray sands with light,
Far off by furthest Rosses
We foot it all the night,
Weaving olden dances
Mingling hands and mingling glances
Till the moon has taken flight;
To and fro we leap
And chase the frothy bubbles,
While the world is full of troubles
And anxious in its sleep.
Come away, O human child!
To the waters and the wild
With a faery, hand in hand,
For the world's more full of weeping than you can understand.
Where the wandering water gushes

From the hills above Glen-Car,
In pools among the rushes
That scarce could bathe a star,
We seek for slumbering trout
And whispering in their ears
Give them unquiet dreams;
Leaning softly out
From ferns that drop their tears
Over the young streams.
Come away, O human child!
To the waters and the wild
With a faery, hand in hand,
For the world's more full of weeping than you can understand.
Away with us he's going,
The solemn-eyed:
He'll hear no more the lowing
Of the calves on the warm hillside
Or the kettle on the hob
Sing peace into his breast,
Or see the brown mice bob
Round and round the oatmeal chest.
For he comes, the human child,
To the waters and the wild
With a faery, hand in hand,
For the world's more full of weeping than he can understand.

OBSERVATIONS

As I mentioned in my introduction, poetry invites—perhaps even demands—interpretation. This piece by Yeats is a classic example because it is one thing on its surface, but the writer invited his readers to make the poem their own. I did. I first encountered "The Stolen Child" in a book of 19th-century poetry found among the countless dusty volumes in my grandmother's house. I was nine.

At first reading, it's a poem about sneaky, nasty little faerie folk who steal children to raise as their own, soothing them by saying their world is less full of pain than the one from which they take the child. However, even as a young boy I sensed that there was more to the piece. I did not fear for the child—and that is not from any lack of empathy. Rather the reverse. I grew up in a household where violence and abuse were common; and in a neighborhood beset with poverty, crime, abuse, and addiction. I grew up, in effect, in darkness. When I read that poem again, I longed to *be* the child stolen by faeries and whisked away to the waters and the wild. That sounded so much safer than a house with a brute of a father and no real way out.

In my real life, I used darkness, distance, solitude, and my grandmother's library as places of safety. Only a year before, when I was eight, I heard Simon & Garfunkel singing about darkness being their friend. It was my friend a lot of time. Not always, but enough to keep me from falling off the edge of the world.

Years later, I went to see Loreena McKennitt in concert and she sang a song whose lyrics were a modified version of Yeats's poem. It recalled those days of childhood hurt and fear, when darkness welcomed me and the spirits who lived in my imagination whispered promises to take me away from the pain of the real world. That made me return to the original poem, and reignited my love for poetry of all kinds, and the poetry of darkness most of all.

Darkness, after all, isn't only where the monsters hide. Often, it's where we hide from the monsters.

Acknowledgments

This project would not have been possible without the assistance of some key folks. My assistant, Dana Fredsti; Marie Whittaker and Kevin J. Anderson of WordFire Press; Eric McHenry—poet and former poet laureate of Kansas; and Lisa Moore, Head of Research Services at Tulane University's Amistad Research Center.

About the Editor

Jonathan Maberry is a *New York Times* bestselling author, #1 Audible bestseller, 5-time Bram Stoker Award winner, four-time Scribe Award winner, Inkpot Award winner, comic book writer, and producer. He is the author of 50 novels, 160 short stories, 16 short story collections, 27 graphic novels, 14 nonfiction books, and has edited 26 anthologies. He is the president of the International Association of Media Tie-in Writers, and editor of *Weird Tales Magazine*. Find him at jonathanmaberry.com.

Other titles by Jonathan Maberry

Empty Graves
Midnight Lullabies
Mystic: The Monk Addison Case Files [coming December, 2024])